MONEY FOR MILLENNIALS

WHY YOUR TWENTIES ARE CRUCIAL FOR
BUILDING FINANCIAL HABITS THAT WILL
BENEFIT YOU A LIFETIME

CRAWFORD IFLAND

CONTENTS

ISBN 978-1-7325857-0-6 (eBook Edition)
ISBN 978-1-7325857-1-3 (Paperback Edition)
Library of Congress Control Number: 2018908433
Printed and bound in the United States of America
First printing August 2018

DISCLAIMER

The information provided in this book is for educational purposes only. It should not be considered legal or financial advice. You should consult with a certified financial adviser and/or tax professional to determine what may be best for your individual needs. The Author is not an investment adviser and does not provide personalized financial advice or act as a financial adviser.

The Author cannot not make any guarantee or other promise as to any results that may be obtained from using this content. No one should make any investment decision without first consulting his or her own financial adviser and conducting his or her own research and due diligence.

To the maximum extent permitted by law, the Author disclaims any and all liability in the event any information, commentary, analysis, opinions, advice and/or recommendations prove to be inaccurate, incomplete or unreliable, or result in any investment or other losses.

———

For more information and resources to help you manage your money better, including a list of the best financial tools to help in your journey, please visit **www.moneyformillennialsbook.com.**

PREFACE

I may only be twenty-six years old, but if you're anything like me, you've read more than your fair share of books on the market relating to personal finance, investing, budgeting, and just about everything in between that promises to reveal the "secrets of the rich" and how you can use personal finance skills to get ahead in life.

In this quest for knowledge about personal finance, I've acquired more than a few books with catchy titles that I quickly discovered were nothing more than get-rich-quick schemes that only improved the personal finances of the author.

Maybe you haven't done these things like I have. Maybe it's just me. Chances are you've read a book like *The Four-Hour Workweek*. Maybe you listen to Dave Ramsey on the radio. Perhaps you took a personal finance class in high school or college (assuming one was offered) in an attempt to gain knowledge, game the system, and end up richer than all of your friends…and that's where you stopped.

And I'm glad you stopped there. The fact is, there's too much bad advice regarding personal finance for Millennials and young twenty-somethings. If I had to take a guess, I bet you've heard at least one of these arguments before:

"Credit cards are the devil! Cut them up and pay only cash!"
"The stock market is going to hell…gold is the only safe investment."
"If you have savings in your twenties, you're doing something wrong."

That last one was the title of an actual article I read recently. My jaw dropped.

If you're smart enough to wade through the heaps of personal finance crap that dominate the news or read sites like BuzzFeed and emerge on the other side unscathed, you're already well on your way to making smarter decisions about money. This book is an attempt to help you on that noble quest.

Why I Wrote This Book

When I reflect on my experience with personal finance in college and beyond, I think about all the mistakes I made: the dumb stuff I bought, the emphasis I placed on the number in my bank account, the unchecked spending and habits I developed over the years that neither served a concrete purpose nor helped me achieve my long-term financial goals.

I'll admit that I'm doing ok with money so far. But I can't help think about how much better I could be doing right now…*if only I had known.*

When I look around at other Millennials, college students, and even older folks who supposedly possess more knowledge and experience on the subject of personal finance, I can't help but think about all the mistakes we make collectively, the bad advice we've been given, and the very real, tangible effects they are having on us – not just on Millennials, but on society at large. Let's face it: our society is terrible with money.

In 2018, the average graduate will emerge from college with more than $47,047 in debt, up nearly 6% from the previous year. The average household has nearly $16,000 in credit card debt and pays more than $904 each year in interest alone. According to a 2013 study by the Federal Reserve, the median retirement account balance in the U.S. was just $59,000. What's worse, according to the National Institute on Retirement Security, almost 40 million American households have no retirement savings at all.

Of course, this isn't 100% a result of poor financial choices. Higher education is becoming more expensive and the Great Recession had a cataclysmic effect that wiped out much of the net worth of many Americans, not to mention the fact that our brains aren't hard-wired to spend much time thinking about – much less planning for – the distant future. But a little education could go a long way. Unfortunately, basic personal finance courses aren't required for most high school or college students.

That's why I wrote this book: I believe that if most people had access to better financial educational resources *when they were young,* they would be far better off. Our society would be more financially healthy, our families stronger, our economy more robust, and our lives a little easier.

Let me be clear: I'm not out to get rich, nor do I suffer from any illusions that this humble attempt to share what I've learned through this book will catapult me to the #1 bestseller list. That's not my goal. Rather, if just one young person reads this book, grows in their knowledge, and feels empowered to make positive changes with their finances, I'll be satisfied.

While I can't mandate that every high schooler in the U.S. complete a basic personal finance course, I realized that I can share what I've learned and compile the best of what others have to say on the subject. The book you're holding in your hands is a result of that effort – an attempt to improve the financial education available to young people, and in turn, to improve our financial future.

Does Anybody Care About Twenty-Somethings?

I'll concede that there *is* indeed good personal finance advice out there if you look hard enough, but we still have a problem on our hands: *most of it is aimed at older audiences.* I'm talking about people on the cusp of buying a home, those who are actively saving for their kids' college educations, and retirees who need to make a fixed income and Social Security benefits last.

But where's the personal financial advice for us? Does anybody have our backs?

As I sat down to research this topic, I quickly noticed two things:

1. Most of the advice out there is bad (or at least misguided).
2. The good advice almost always comes from companies who are trying to sell you something.

Since you're holding this book in your hands, I'm going to make a few bold assumptions about you:

1. I'm assuming you're smart;

2. I'm assuming you you want to be proactive and take your financial future in your own hands;
3. I'm assuming that you don't want to hear the same advice being peddled elsewhere; and
4. I'm assuming that you don't want to be marketed or sold to.

Cold calls from telemarketers are rarely welcome, and I'm guessing that you don't want financial companies trying to sell you on their products, so this book won't make an attempt to do so either. You will encounter suggestions for different personal finance apps to try and investment resources to utilize, but your own financial journey is just that – *yours.* I'm just trying to share what has been helpful to me, but you're not obligated to use any of the products or services I recommend. The last thing I want is for you to feel like you're being sold to when you came here to learn.

Also, a disclaimer: I am by no means an expert on personal finance. I still make mistakes and dumb decisions with money sometimes. We all do – from the college student to the most seasoned hedge fund manager, we have all made financial choices we regret. Despite my mistakes, I've been fortunate enough to start two businesses from my dorm room in college, work for clients around the world (which has involved international travel), buy a house when I was 23, and have a significant amount already saved for retirement. Through this book, I'll do my best to help you make the most of your financial life in your twenties, just as I have.

If you were expecting this book to be full of financial advice from some stodgy business guy with multiple acronyms after their name, I'd recommend you look elsewhere. But if you're like me and you want a simple way to properly manage your finances when you're young *so that you have better opportunities when you're older*, I think you'll enjoy this book.

Why Did You Buy this Book?

The way I see it, you bought this book for one of three reasons:

1. You want to get rich;
2. You want to experience less stress when it comes to the topic of your finances;
3. You want to set yourself up for success further down the road; or
4. All of the above.

While most of us have a propensity for liking nice things (and while there's nothing wrong with living a comfortable life-style), I don't think becoming "rich" by the world's standards should be the primary goal. In the history of humankind, perhaps no other desire has destroyed and distorted so many people and societies than has the pursuit of wealth for wealth's sake.

I went to college in a particularly wealthy enclave of Southern California, where it wasn't unusual to see Bentleys and Aston-Martins on my way from my dorm room to my favorite coffee shop downtown. Our school itself was surrounded by huge – and I mean *huge* – estates of the rich and famous. Movie stars, Fortune 500 CEOs, Oprah, you name it: everyone who was anyone had a home there (Or two. Or three). On the outside, they had it all: year-round perfect weather, gorgeous homes, fast sports cars, "the good life" that so many dream of…

And yet, as I looked around, I saw so many people who weren't satisfied. They were surrounded by all the material possessions and money in the world, but they just didn't look *happy.* (Maybe it's the fact that their bodies were 95% plastic. I don't know.) After spending four years at school surrounded by so much wealth, I could see that the childhood desire of many – to "be rich" – wasn't all it was cracked up to be.

One of the most vivid memories I have in college was in the Spring of my Junior year, on the second-to-last day of Spring Break. A group of us had just returned from Haiti, where our entrepreneurship class gave seven Haitian locals micro-loans to help them start their own businesses. It was a life-changing week for so many reasons, but the most challenging thought I experienced didn't happen in Haiti, but shortly after we landed at LAX. After a long eighteen hours of travel, we were almost home. As we crested the hill into one of the most expensive ZIP codes in the country, the quiet voice of my friend piped up from the back of the bus: *"Well, there's a juxtaposition for you."*

At first I wondered what she had meant, but then it dawned on me: less than 24 hours prior, we had been in the poorest region in the Western Hemisphere, and now we were crossing into one of the wealthiest areas of one of the wealthiest nations on the face of the planet.

In that moment, I realized the emptiness that comes from the unbridled pursuit of money. Here, surrounded by the sprawling estates of the mega-wealthy, was so much emptiness. But in Haiti, where earning $2 a day meant you had "made it," we saw true contentment and joy.

It may sound cliche, and I'm fine with that. What I learned that day is that money should be a *tool,* not the goal. Who on earth said that being rich was the be-all-end-all goal of life? I don't think it is. Yes, that's what our culture teaches, but who says we have to believe it? I think that too often, money gets in the way of living a truly rich life – whether there's too much of it or not enough. Maybe a desire to be rich is the motivation behind why you bought this book. That's fine. But that's not really what this book is about.

It's also quite possible that you're reading this book so that you can learn to stress less about money. According to *Forbes*, one in four Americans have PTSD-like symptoms from financial stress. Among Millennials, that number jumps to 36% – more than one in three. As I did research for this book, I surveyed nearly one hundred twenty-somethings about the state of their personal finances: how much student debt they had, how much money they had been able to save, what personal finance topics they were most curious about. One of the questions in the survey dealt with how worried they were about money. And you know what I found out?

On a scale of zero to ten (zero being "I never worry about money," and ten being "I worry about money every day"), most people responded that they were a 7 – that they frequently worried about money. If that's you, rest assured that you're not alone. Especially when we're young and just starting out, it's common for us to think about money a lot:

Will I be able to scrape together enough for next month's rent?
How am I going to repay so much student debt?
My job doesn't pay that well…am I ever going to earn more?
What if I lose my job entirely?

My goal is to help you quell these fears and stress less. While there's no one "magic bullet" that will catapult you to financial success overnight, adopting a smart approach to your financial health can help you reach your goals and slowly add more margin into your life.

The third and final reason I suspect you bought this book is that you want to be proactive, to learn how to set yourself up for success farther down the road. There are so many reasons why we would want to do this: maybe you want to retire comfortably in a larger house or travel the world when you're sixty. Maybe investing in your future kids' and grandkids' education is the most important thing to you. Perhaps you want to make the wisest decisions with your money now to avoid adopting your parents' attitudes toward money because they were always stressed and they didn't save early enough, wondering if they were going to have enough for retirement, etc. All of those are good reasons.

I saw an amusing video recently. It was a replication of the famous "The Marshmallow Test," a psychological experiment in which young children were seated in front of a plate with a single marshmallow on it. The children were told by the supervising adult that they could eat the marshmallow when the adult left the room, but if they waited until the adult came back into the room several minutes later, they would get *two* marshmallows to enjoy.

You can imagine the results - the effort of the kids trying to exercise self-control is just too funny to put into words. (If you're so inclined, you can watch the video for yourself). Isn't that hilarious? See how much effort and willpower it takes for these kids to delay gratification and get two marshmallows instead of one? You almost feel the kids' pain as you see the consternation on their faces, struggling to delay gratification in the hopes of receiving more.

And so it is with us and money. It's easy to laugh at the video and say, "I'd never do that. I'd be patient and diligent." But on the inside, aren't we all like little kids lusting after a fluffy, delicious marshmallow?

This struggle with self-control isn't unique to twenty-somethings. Chances are that your parents, older siblings, or friends (regardless of their age) struggle with delayed gratification in some form or fashion. It may be money, it may be a career, kids, you name it – we're all susceptible.

For twenty-somethings just starting out, money is often the temptation. Burdened with student debt and the prospect of never finding your "dream job" in a new city that's all-too-expensive to live in, it's quite easy for young people to stress about money – and even easier to give in to its temptation by splurging your most recent paycheck on a new outfit or a round of drinks for your friends. *Why do you think the average credit card debt for twenty-somethings is more than $3,718?*

In this book, we'll examine how to use your finances wisely in your twenties and beyond. By knowing how the pieces of your financial life fit together – and by using that knowledge to your advantage – you'll be well on your way to greater levels of financial health and freedom.

A Word About the Word "Millennial"

When writing this book, I encountered something time and time again – so often, in fact, that it is worth addressing before we continue: the word "Millennial" is somewhat divisive.

Broadly defined, Millennials are young adults who were born between 1980 – 2000 (give or take – there is no set definition). We've been accused of "killing" countless industries, from beer and napkins to cereal and even golf (although last time I checked, all of these things still exist). We've been labeled as entitled, lazy, and unwilling to work. And while some of these assertions may correct about a select few in our generation, I believe it is irresponsible to label an entire group as such. Not every Millennial is entitled (and not every Millennial hates napkins).

For every article online claiming that Millennials have "killed" another industry, there's another source to refute it. Statistics and opinions about Millennials abound, but it's hard to ascertain exactly how representative of our generation these facts actually are. Millennials are the least understood generation in recent memory. Perhaps we should stop making assumptions about Millennials' behavior as a *group* and focus instead on the wise decisions we can make as *individuals* in our twenties – decisions that, en masse, could reverse the negative stereotypes about our age group. It's my hope that this book can play a small part in such a transformation.

I realize that the title of this book, *Money for Millennials*, may be "offensive" to some who don't wish to associate with this generation and would never use such a label to describe themselves. However, for those with an extreme aversion to the label "Millennial," this book is still for you.

For this reason, I feel it is necessary to preface the rest of this book by saying this: when I refer to "Millennials," I am not referring to the lazy, entitled stereotype of a generation the media would make us out to be. I'm addressing a broader group of people, namely those in their high school years to those in their twenties and early thirties. This book is for those who want to take advantage of the available time they have in their youth to wisely invest, diligently save, and smartly navigate the next move so that later on they can have two marshmallows instead of one.

Decisions matter, especially over the long run. Through this book, we'll explore how you can make the very best decisions with your finances now so that you reap the outsized benefits farther down the road – *regardless of whether you call yourself a "Millennial" or not.*

PART I

OUR RELATIONSHIP
WITH MONEY

Chapter 1

UNDERSTANDING TIME

YOU'RE ALREADY A MILLIONAIRE. YOU JUST
DON'T KNOW IT YET

L et's begin with an observation so blatantly obvious that
it may seem a bit offensive to your intelligence: our
culture is obsessed with money.

In modern American society, there's no escaping the unbridled desire for money. It's everywhere you turn. The media extols
it. Celebrities flaunt it. It's pervasive in pop culture. The Top 40
can't stop singing its praises. As Chris Brown says in his song
Look At Me Now, "I get what you get in ten years...*in two days.*"
Our own president is a billionaire, for goodness sake. To an
outsider, it would seem that we've made money the chief end of
our existence. We just can't get enough.

The love of money isn't confined to the adult world, either. It
starts at an early age. Although children have nearly no expenses
and very few things on which to spend their allowance or hard-
earned lawn-mowing profits, they begin to adopt their parents'
attitudes towards money from an early age. Deep down, adults
know that their kids – like nearly everyone in society – will face
struggles with money, but it all seems too ephemeral...so they

teach their kids a thing or two, but if they are being honest, they don't think that what they teach their young children about money really matters all that much.

In reality, it has profound significance.

A key way children learn is by watching adults and their behaviors. When children witness adults' attitudes regarding money, wealth, and spending habits, they subconsciously adopt many of the same behaviors and attitudes. Americans (unknowingly) teach their kids from an early age that money equals status and power. It may never be explicitly mentioned, but it is inferred, and as a result, many children grow up believing that money is the be-all-end-all goal. Research has shown that childrens' financial habits are more or less established by the time they turn seven, a fact that has serious implications for the financial well-being of the next generation.

In a recent study performed in the United Kingdom, 1,300 parents asked their children about their career aspirations. The children were not provided a list of answers to choose from; rather, they answered on their own. When asked what they would like to be when they grow up, one in five children under the age of 10 years old said they didn't care what they did for a career – they "just wanted to be rich." As part of the study, parents were also told to ask their children whether they thought money could buy happiness. Nearly 8 out of 10 youngsters said "yes."

To some degree, money can provide material goods and services that increase the quality of our lives, but the attitude that modern society reinforces in our children is disconcerting. Perhaps most disturbingly, we're not teaching the next generation smart financial habits.

Chalk it up to money being a "taboo" topic, or to widespread financial illiteracy among adults or a perceived fear among parents that their own poor financial choices will lessen their clout and reputation in their children's eyes. As a society, we don't discuss money – and it's having a severe impact on our children. On an international test of personal finance skills given in 2013, students in the United States fared worse than their peers in Poland, Australia, and Shanghai, China and scored about average for students in developed countries.

Unfortunately, the story about personal finance doesn't get better when youngsters mature and enter the workforce. For starters, many young adults can't answer the most basic personal finance questions. The National Longitudinal Survey of Youth asked young Americans three basic questions about money:

1. Suppose you had $100 in a savings account and the interest rate was 2% per year. After 5 years, how much do you think you would have in the account if you let the money grow: more than $102, exactly $102, or less than $102?

2. Imagine that the interest rate on your savings account was 1% per year and inflation was 2% per year. After 1 year, would you be able to buy more than, exactly the same as, or less than today with the money in this account?

3. Do you think that the following statement is true or false? "Buying a single company stock usually provides a safer return than a stock mutual fund."

Only 27% of young adults in this study answered all three questions correctly. *(The correct answers are "more than $102," "less than today," and "false.")*

It's clear from these findings that a love for money is near universal but our knowledge of personal finance is lacking. Maybe you find yourself in this situation. Maybe your parents' attitudes towards money have shaped your attitudes, regardless of whether your financial education as a kid was explicitly taught or implicitly witnessed.

If you're in that boat, you're not alone. Many of us have unrealistic expectations and attitudes about money. Some stem from our parents' unhealthy habits; others come from a lack of proper financial education in our youth. Regardless of the source, learning how to have a proper understanding of money – and a proper relationship with it – is a key skill that we so desperately need.

So what are we to do? If we want to be more financially successful than previous generations and not make the mistakes of our parents, what is the best path forward? Actually, forget success for a moment – if we want to be more financially *healthy* than older generations or our peers, how should we then proceed? The importance of a proper financial education from an early age cannot be understated. It's never too late to begin forming more healthy financial habits, but for those of us whose habits and attitudes towards money are more or less developed by now, what can we do?

I would contend that if we want to become more financially healthy, we must begin by reframing our expectations and desires about money. We may not have been served well by parents, society, or our educational system up to this point, but if we want to be successful going forward, the onus is on us. It is only when we educate ourselves to view money in the correct light that we will be able to adopt a wise perspective and healthy habits regarding its acquisition and use.

To kick off our exploration of money, *what if I told you that you were already a millionaire?*

Congrats: You're a millionaire. You just don't know it yet.

I have a confession to make: this chapter isn't actually about money. I suppose the chapter title is a bit misleading, but to enhance our exploration of money and healthy personal finance habits in your twenties, we're going to begin by talking about a more valuable – and more scarce – resource available to you.

If you read the preface, you'll know that I studied economics & business in college. What I didn't tell you is that many of my business classes were taught by none other than…my father. He came off the Board of Trustees at my alma mater to fill a gap in the economics & business department halfway through my sophomore year. At first, I thought it would be weird having my dad walking around campus (especially as he gained a reputation for his hard grading as he began doling out grades to my peers). In reality, it was a ton of fun. His focus was on upper-division business electives, including Entrepreneurship and New Venture Development, Executive Leadership, and others.

So there I was, in uncharted territory: my father for a professor. The last semester of my Senior year found me sitting in Senior Seminar, the capstone course of our education in the economics & business department. One day to begin the class, he proudly announced to a packed class full of Seniors, ready to head out into the real world: *"I'm going to let you in on a little secret: everyone in this room is a millionaire."*

Cue the confused looks.

Here we sat, with only a few weeks in the semester until we

graduated, wide-eyed and terrified, and the vast majority of us about to emerge from college as NINJAs. If the statistics on student debt were to be believed, each of us would have an average of more than $37,000 in debt when we walked across the stage to receive our diplomas. As is the case for so many undergrads, many students in the room were anxiously anticipating moving home for a year or two to save money before applying to grad school. Very few of us had a concrete plan for the next six months, let alone having any real job prospects lined up. *How on earth could we be millionaires?*

As puzzled faces looked around the classroom to make sure everyone else was just as confused as they were, a few were bold enough to raise their hands and question that statement:

"Umm, I don't even have a job right now."
"I mean, I have a savings account, but last time I checked, a million has a few more zeroes in it than my balance does…"

My dad conceded that our bank accounts may not have that number of zeroes in it, and that our entry-level jobs were not likely to provide a salary anywhere close to what would be required to become a millionaire anytime soon. However, he stood by his belief that we were still millionaires…and he proceeded to tell us that he was jealous of our place in life. *Huh?*

Standing in the front of the room was a professor who had a successful 30-year business career and was now teaching at one of the best (and most expensive) liberal arts colleges in the nation… and he was telling us how jealous he was of our position in life? How, as he claimed, could we be so incredibly rich yet not even realize it?

The conversation that followed was enlightening. As it turns out, when he referred to us as rich, he wasn't talking about being rich in the conventional sense of the word – rich with money – he was talking about being rich with *time.*

Every single student in the room that day was what my Dad liked to call a *time millionaire.* Besides the obvious commitments of class, practice, and homework, we possessed nearly unlimited disposable time in college to do what we pleased. Many of us spent our time in the traditional ways of most college students: studying, working out, reading that chemistry textbook for the hundredth time in the library in an attempt to eke out an extra 1% in our final exam grade, you name it.

Beyond school work and other commitments, we filled our days with everything else that college students do: going to the beach, sleeping in, watching a movie on a Friday night, working a part-time job, etc. Nothing out of the ordinary for us. Nothing special. But to someone older like him, the freedom afforded to us by nearly unlimited amounts of time is a luxury that made us rich beyond measure.

In college, it certainly didn't feel that way – there were always more things to do than there were hours in the day. Overcommitment is a pandemic on the modern American campus. But his point was profound, and it stuck with me: high schoolers, college students, and twenty somethings like us have an enormous advantage over older folks with the commitments of work, family, and social engagements. We're so rich with time, but we don't even realize it.

You might not want to go around telling everyone you're a millionaire. However, if you're under the age of 30 (especially if you're unmarried, still in school, or living at home or in a cheap apartment with friends), you should embrace this fact internally: ***you are a time millionaire, and at this point in your life, being*** *rich with time is far more important than being rich with money.*

Time is Money? Depends on Who You Ask.

Certain cultural expectations exist within any society. One of these oh-so-prevalent expectations is that when you're young, you don't have a lot of money. Ever heard the song *Young, Dumb, and Broke* on the radio? My point exactly. Blame it on the rising price of higher education, fewer job opportunities, or the fact that "grad school is the new college" – it doesn't matter. The fact is, when we're young, we usually don't have a lot of money…but we do possess a lot of time.

You've probably heard it said that *time is money,* but this isn't an objective truth. The relationship between time and money is better thought of as a sliding scale. The value you put on your time or your money – and the habits you adopt regarding their use – may look very different than my values.

But let's generalize. Most often by necessity, Millennials and twenty-somethings can – and do – trade time for money; unfortunately, when we're young and possess inordinate amounts of time, we tend to value our time as fairly cheap. The vast majority of those in older generations expect twenty-somethings to be poor, and that's ok. There's a reason why everyone refers to newly married people in their early- to mid-twenties as "poor newlyweds" - *it's to be expected.* Fast forward a few decades, a few kids, a mortgage and the increasingly demanding responsibilities that come with moving up the corporate ladder, and you'll realize that as life gets busier, time really *is* money.

There's an interesting relationship here. Those in older generations generally have more money than time, and those younger than them (again, speaking in generalities) have more time than money. As we age, we tend to see a shift in these resources: the number in our bank account increases (hopefully), but the time available to us seems to dwindle away. Everyone on the face of the planet gets the same 24 hours in a day, but for some people, it never seems like enough. For those people whose careers, families, or other commitments demand a lot of their time, time is much more valuable than money. To put it in economist-speak, the marginal value of one additional unit of time is far greater than the marginal value of one additional unit of money.

For others, including younger people like us, money tends to be much more valuable than time. It's a simple equation:

When we're young:
In terms of *quantity*, money < time.
In terms of *value*, money > time.

When we're older:
In terms of *quantity*, money > time.
In terms of *value*, money < time.

Despite your lack of a substantial net worth as a twenty-something, when older people look at you, they tend to be jealous because you possess an abundance of what they most desire: time. If you're reading this and you're still in college, you're especially rich. You will graduate soon, and once you take on the commitment of a full-time job, it's going to feel like you have *zero* time any longer. For most people in our society, this phenomenon only gets worse with age.

There's a scene in the movie *Wall Street: Money Never Sleeps,* in which multi-millionaire financial titan Gordon Gekko says to a young trader (played by Charlie Sheen), *"If there's one thing I've learned, it's that money is not the prime commodity in our lives. Time is the most valuable commodity I know."*

There's a valuable lesson there: time is much more precious and valuable than we recognize.

Time: The Great Equalizer

Want me to let you in on a little secret? Even though your parents, your grandparents, your boss (whoever, really) may have substantially more money than you do and seem to be "better off," you have an advantage.

That's right: in one key way, you're better off than they are. There's a distinct way to use the limited financial resources you have to level the playing field so that you can be in a far better position when you're their age – not only better off than you are now, but better off than *they are* now.

In our twenties, we're faced with many options when it comes to wisely allocating the limited amount of dollars we have left over once we've provided for our everyday needs: should we tackle our student loans? Pay down credit cards? Invest in the stock market? Save for a down payment on a house?

No matter how you decide to manage your finances, the key is to start now. I'm not going to say that it doesn't matter what you do with your money (it does) but it matters less *what* you do with it, and more that you're doing *something* with it.

At this point in your life, time is the greatest asset you have. Time is your distinct advantage. And if you're not actively using that time to your advantage, you're wasting the biggest opportunity you'll have. From compounding interest to investments, saving for retirement, or even putting aside a small amount into savings each month, there's no substitute for time – and there's no way to recover it once it's gone.

Or think about it in terms of risk: putting the small amount of money you have into the stock market at such a young age *feels* risky. We tell ourselves that we'll do that when we're older and have more of a financial cushion. But what happens? We get married, have a kid or two, acquire a mortgage and car payments, and there's not very much left over after all. Plus, we have a tendency to raise our standard of living when we advance in our careers. And what have we missed out on that we'll *never* be able to get back? Time.

As my dad liked to tell his students, most things that feel risky as a college student or young adult aren't risky at all. In the grand scheme of things, he would compare us to babies in diapers: if we screwed up, we didn't have that far to fall, our butts were padded anyways, and most of the mess is contained inside the diaper. *So why not take the risk?*

Let's take investing for retirement, for example. More than 43% of twenty-somethings I surveyed when writing this book didn't have retirement savings at all, even though a retirement plan might be available through their work. Most twenty-some-things think it's too early to start saving for retirement, and I can't say that I blame them. At such a young age, the financial discipline to save for retirement seems too thoughtful, too rational. But in fact, the opposite is true. Because of the effects of compound interest, one of the biggest factors influencing how much money you'll have available when you retire isn't necessarily *how much* you saved, but *how early* you started saving it.

Take this as an example: suppose you're 23 years old. You make $45,000 a year and set aside 10% of your earnings for retirement with every paycheck. No matter what happens, you remain devoted to this goal: you never miss a payment, you resist the temptation to withdraw your money, and you let it accumulate over time. With an average market return of 6% over the next 42 years until you retire (the historical average rate of return is 6.8%), you'll have approximately $532,653 to fund your retirement.

But what if you don't start saving until you're 26? A difference of three years couldn't make that much of a difference, could it?

Turns out that it does: by just delaying retirement savings by three years, you'll have $456,794 compared to more than $530,000. *That's a difference of more than $73,000 – just for starting a few years earlier.* Assuming your income stays the same, over the course of those three years you would have contributed $13,500. But over the course of time, thanks to the power of compound interest, you'll have earned an extra $60,000 – essentially for free. Wouldn't you rather have an extra $73,000 sitting around when you retire? I know I would.

So if you want to level the playing field when it comes to personal finance in your twenties, you need to start now. We'll get into in-depth strategies in later chapters, but whatever you do, don't wait - *do it now.*

The Magic of Compounding

In the example above, the reason for the $73,000 difference is compound interest. Albert Einstein said (perhaps apocryphally) that *"compound interest is the eighth wonder of the world. He who understands it, earns it; he who doesn't...pays it."*

Origins aside, that quote is both powerful and true. There's nothing quite like compound interest to help you reach your financial goals, and there's no substitute for starting early. I've said it before, and I'll say it again: the most influential factor in deciding whether you reach long-term financial goals isn't how much you make or how much you save – it's when you start.

Compound interest is a powerful force that levels the playing field. Thanks to compound interest, a 22-year-old who makes $45,000 a year and diligently saves can be better prepared for retirement than a 55-year-old who makes $200,000 a year and has high expenses to match but no saving habit or plan. Sure, one lifestyle looks more glamorous, but what's important: appearances, or actual financial health?

Understanding compound interest is vital to establishing healthy financial habits and realizing your financial goals. It's the most important mental model you should pursue and the number one way to build your wealth over time.

Nearly everything we'll explore throughout the rest of this book relies on a solid understanding of compound interest. It is one of the major "building blocks" in the foundation. If you "get" compound interest and put it into practice, you'll be well on your way to real financial freedom.

Shifting The Mindset

To be honest, the hardest part of learning good financial habits is the effort it takes to shift your mindset. Figuring out the differences between Roth and Traditional IRAs, analyzing a company's financials, and crunching the numbers in your budget is easy; learning (and practicing) good financial habits, especially when temptations are so present and easily accessible, is *hard, hard work*. But it is achievable. It just requires a shift in your mindset.

Not only is this hard work, but on the surface it's not particularly appealing, either. Modern culture preaches a gospel of instant gratification: buy whatever you want, put it on your credit card, and don't worry about it. Don't think about whether you have the money to pay for it; forget about the true cost when you factor interest in – *you deserve it!*

Instant gratification is easy, but the returns offered by such an ethos are temporal and unsatisfying at best, destructive at worst. To succeed in matters of personal finance (especially at a young age), you must adopt a longer-term mindset and be willing to forego today's desires for tomorrow's goals. It takes saying "no" to appealing opportunities and distractions now so that you may have more bandwidth to respond to future opportunities.

We've discussed compound interest and its importance as a foundational tool of personal finance, but delayed gratification is just as important. The ability to delay one's desires and adopt a long-term mindset is perhaps the most vital combination you can implement. It's crucial to get this right at an early age – there's simply no replacement for having a solid foundation on which to build. In the moment, delayed gratification ain't fun, but it's a crucial skill that will reap dividends throughout your life.

Begin with Strategy

We'll get into many of the tactics for building wealth and wisely using money in later chapters. For now, the most appropriate next step is to take an expository look at the foundational, strategic mindset that makes personal financial success possible. Clichés abound: without a strong foundation, even the most beautiful structure will crumble; a team is only as strong as its weakest member; a home can't stand without a solid foundation. Likewise, if you don't develop healthy financial habits, all the financial knowledge in the world won't help you achieve your goals. Strategy and fundamentals must always come first.

In finance and life in general, a thorough understanding of where you stand is the first step in your journey. We must begin with a valid assessment of our current situation in order to know how to reach our destination; the roadmap will become evident along the way. If you don't want your life to look like everyone else's when you're forty, you have to stop *acting* like everyone else when you're twenty.

As with any good strategy, you also have to know where you want to end up in order to figure out how to get there. For the quarterback, the goal is to lead his team to victory. For the CEO, it's to build a successful business that delivers value to its customers and earns shareholders a good return.

For the young twenty-something like you, a good goal could be any number of things: paying off student loans, buying a car, getting out from under excessive credit card debt, learning how to invest in the stock market…the list goes on and on.

Many personal finance guides attempt to prescribe goals to their readers, claiming that building a solid retirement portfolio or viciously reducing all forms of debt is the formula for success. This book is a little different. I won't insult your intelligence by claiming to know what's good for you or by prescribing solutions for your financial health without knowing your exact situation. You're smart. You can figure it out.

I want to give you a basic understanding of the core concepts and tools necessary to succeed with money and build healthy financial habits. Whether that's paying down debt or saving for a house, it doesn't matter – if you have the right skills, you'll know what to do. The goals are up to you.

Before You Move On

One other note: I conclude each chapter with a brief "home-work" section. These sections are intended to be brief exercises – five minutes or less – to help you take control of your financial situation using the knowledge you attained in the chapter you just read.

So, it's homework time: take out a piece of paper, jot a note on your phone, whatever – but take some time to think about these three timelines:

THIS WEEK

We talked a lot about time in this chapter, specifically the benefits of building healthy financial habits when you're young and using the power of compound interest to your advantage.

Do a brief audit of where you spend your time on a daily basis. Is there anything that can be reduced or cut out? Netflix? Browsing social media? Try to find an hour of "wasted" time in your week, and brainstorm a few ways that you could repurpose it to achieve your goals.

Your use of this newfound time doesn't have to be financial – it could be spent on anything. You could use it to go over your spending, but you could also devote an extra hour at the gym, research credit cards, or go to the beach and spend an hour in silence letting yourself relax. The goal here isn't to spend that hour obsessing about money (or thinking about anything financial, for that matter), but to begin *transforming your relationship with your time and how you use it.* Shifts in mindset don't just happen overnight – they're like muscles that must be exercised. Taking control of just one hour of time this week and repurposing it to serve your long-term goals will help you see how you spend your time in a new way.

This Month

Specifically as it pertains to personal finance, where do you want to be a month from now, and what steps will you take to get there? Do you want to have opened your first credit card (if you don't have one already)? Do you want to set a goal to make more than the minimum payment on your student loans and try to make that habit sustainable? Pick one "bigger-ticket item" that you'd like to cross off your list in the next 30 days and write it down. Check in at the end of each week to see how you're progressing towards your goal. Create a calendar event on your phone to remind you to check back in next month and see how you did.

You don't necessarily have to *accomplish* this goal in the next 30 days, but you should make some progress towards the goal you choose. Again, it's the habit-building that matters, not the goal itself.

Next Year

Similarly to the monthly goal, think to yourself: where do you want to be a year from now? Financially, what would you like to have accomplished? Do you want to have saved enough money to buy a used car? Pay off all your credit cards? Grow your savings account to $5,000 (or more)?

It doesn't matter what the goal is, just that you have one.

Write it down. Create a recurring calendar event to remind yourself to check in at the end of every month and assess your progress, adjusting if necessary.

————

Now that we've taken a look at the power of time, compounding, and how to use them to your advantage, we'll turn our attention to a vital element of our economy that is often misunderstood: credit.

Chapter 2

USING CREDIT WISELY

THE DEFINITIVE GUIDE ON HOW NOT TO BE
AN IDIOT

Alright, now to the fun part: learning the ins and outs of personal finance.

Credit – and especially credit cards – can be a polarizing topic, especially among those who call themselves personal finance "experts." Some love credit cards; others hate them. Some people live by credit cards, using them to pay for every expense on a daily basis (I'm one of these people, for reasons I'll explain below). Others hardly ever use credit cards, preferring to pay cash for everything. Still other people swear that credit cards are an evil byproduct of greedy corporations who are out to destroy the moral fabric of America.

Regardless of what you may have heard (or believe) about credit cards, there are a few things you to need to know in order to build credit responsibly. Like it or not, our society revolves around credit, so if you want to build healthy financial habits, credit will play a part in your financial life.

When it comes to credit, there's so much bad advice out there that it's nauseating. If we are to have a serious discussion about the responsible use of credit, we must first clear the air and dispel some popular myths about credit and credit cards, to set the record straight.

Myth #1: You Don't Need Credit

It's almost shameful to consider how many people out there claim you don't need credit. From the payday lenders with bars on the windows to sketchy used car dealerships and obnoxious TV ads (*"BAD CREDIT? NO CREDIT? NO PROBLEM!"*), we've been inundated by those claiming that credit isn't important, that we can get by without it.

But more often than not, anyone who claims that credit isn't important has a very real incentive to get you to believe it. These parties are trying to keep you in the dark about credit in order to profit from the fact that you have bad credit, or worse – none at all. They're using you, and the sooner you know this, the sooner you can use this knowledge to your advantage by beating them at their own game.

If you want to make a large purchase at any point in your lifetime – say, a house or a car – and you can't pay cash, you're going to need credit. It's just a fact of life. Unless you want to buy used cars in terrible condition for the rest of your life (and likely overpay for them), you're going to need credit. Unless you've a few hundred thousand dollars lying around and can pay cash for a house, you're going to need credit. Despite the James Bond-like sex appeal of showing up to a home closing with a suitcase full of $100 bills, credit is a more useful way to make such a large purchase.

Ok, so it *is* technically possible to make significant purchases (think: a car) without good credit, but it's generally a bad idea. There are two main reasons why:

1. *THE QUALITY OF THE GOODS YOU CAN BUY WITHOUT CREDIT IS GENERALLY SUBPAR.*

Sure, you could buy a car with bad credit, but you likely won't be driving a reliable car, I can tell you that. Say hello to a 1997 Honda Civic with 234,000 miles on it.

2. *YOU WILL LIKELY PAY EXORBITANTLY HIGH INTEREST RATES.*

When you have good credit, you qualify for lower interest rates. Although a few percentage points (or even partial percentage points) don't seem like a big deal, it can literally cost you thousands of dollars (or more, depending on the size of your purchase) over the long-term. It's a much better position to have good credit than to have poor credit or no credit at all.

I read an article recently about predatory payday lenders, and what I learned shocked me. For millions of Americans who have bad (or no) credit and need cash fast, a payday lender can seem to be the only available option. In exchange for a small short-term loan (the average amount is $350), a customer agrees to pay a flat fee and allows the lender access to the customer's bank account for the duration of the loan. What seems like a small amount – usually $10 or $15 per $100 borrowed – can amount to an annualized rate of *more than 400%.*

Compare that to current interest rates for car loans for people with decent credit (4.5%) and mortgages (4.1%), and the penalty you pay for lack of credit is exorbitant and appalling. As the author of one book puts it, "One of the great ironies in modern

America is that the less money you have, the more you pay to use it."

Myth #2: Credit Cards are Evil

If you're mired in credit card debt, you know the full effect of the ridiculously high interest rates that come with paying anything less than the full balance. As of 2014, 34% of American households carried a balance on one or more credit cards, subjecting themselves to these high interest rates.

Resentment of credit card companies is fairly high, just slightly below Osama bin Laden or Adolf Hitler on the likability scale. Depending on how badly you've been burned, you may put *money in general* in the evil pile. If you did, you wouldn't be alone…but you would be wrong. And I wouldn't blame you.

Millions of people around the world (especially twenty-somethings fresh out of college) have been devastated by credit card debt. This phenomenon isn't particularly new, but it has caused financial "experts" to preach dramatic ultimatums and spread dangerous rhetoric about credit cards.

Speaking of credit card use, one of the most well-known personal finance personalities today said, *"Responsible use of a credit card does not exist."* It's not hard to understand where he's coming from: for those enrolled in his financial freedom courses, this may be sound advice. He has helped countless individuals emerge from their mountains of debt and establish positive, healthy financial habits. That's an incredibly positive thing, and much of his advice is solid – *when it's correctly aimed at an audience who struggles with self-control.* After all, many of his students find themselves in one of his courses *because* of irresponsible credit card use.

But for those who are able to use a credit card wisely, his advice is terrible. Credit cards are not evil, and despite what personal finance "experts" would have you believe, there is a responsible way to use them.

The important thing to remember about credit cards is that they're a *tool* – what matters is how you use them. By themselves, credit cards are morally neutral; it's the person using or abusing them who knows whether they are a positive or negative thing. Just as the Internet can be used as a tool for good (to communicate instantaneously, share ideas, and connect people) or for bad (to perpetuate scams, spread pornography, or conduct illegal activities), so can credit cards. When used wisely to build credit and to set yourself up for financial success, they are unparalleled in their benefits; when used to drive yourself into debt up to your eyeballs, they can destroy your future and lop a few years off your life due to the overwhelming stress of debt repayment. It's your choice.

MYTH #3: THERE'S NO POSITIVE SIDE TO CREDIT CARD USE

If you listen to what mainstream media says about using a credit card, you might believe this myth. Looking at the statistics about credit card debt in America, it's no surprise that we're a bit wary of the plastic in our wallets:

- *As of 2017, the average American family has more than $15,983 in credit card debt. That represents more than $931 billion that credit card companies in the U.S. are going to collect someday.*
- *38% of American households have credit card debt or other forms of consumer debt.*

- *The average U.S. household is more than $133,568 in debt (this includes things like mortgage debt and student debt, but credit cards make up a large percentage of this number).*
- *The average household is paying a total of $904 in interest on credit card debt per year.*
- *We're ashamed of our credit card debt: as of 2013, actual lender-reported credit card debt was 155% greater than borrower-reported balances.*
- *We don't like to talk about our credit card debt. In a March 2013 CreditCards.com poll, 85% of respondents said they were unlikely or somewhat unlikely to talk with a stranger about credit card debt -- a subject more taboo than religion, politics, salary and love life details. As one article puts it, "financial impotence has many of the characteristics of sexual impotence, not least of which is the desperate need to mask it."*

While those statistics aren't 100% accurate across the board (some families don't use credit cards, while plenty of people are what's called "transactors," meaning they pay off their full balance each month), there are some assumptions we can make about the relationship most Americans have with their credit cards. Taking our collective debt balances into account, most Americans don't understand the long-term financial impacts of their decision to swipe their plastic at the register. It feels good at the time, but that's because most people aren't thinking about the true cost of their purchases. That leads us to an uncomfortable conclusion: most Americans are irresponsible with their credit cards.

As we've seen, financial experts are quick to decry any and all credit card use as irresponsible, but that's not fair to the millions of Americans who *do* use their credit cards wisely. When they say "there is no positive side to credit card use," they're really assuming two things about their audience:

1. *They are not smart enough to use a credit card; and*
2. *They don't need credit.*

Both of these assumptions are unfair. Responsible use of a credit card is not a black box – it's something that can be learned. Like any skill, it takes diligence and self-regulation to master. Yes, plenty of people lack self-control and haven't developed the healthy financial habits necessary to use a credit card responsibly, but that doesn't mean they can't learn.

Credit cards aren't scary, evil, or an instrument of Satan…it's just that many people just don't know how to use them responsibly (or can't seem to control their impulses). Research has shown time and time again that it's very hard for people to envision the impacts their current choices will have on their future selves. We're not wired to think about an uncertain future by default. But it is a skill that can – and must – be learned if we are to succeed financially.

Understanding Credit

At its core, credit isn't very hard to understand. Let's say you want to obtain a credit card. When you apply for credit, the issuing financial institution will look at your financial health, including your current income, your debts, and other factors. Seeing that you're "worthy" of a loan, they will extend a certain amount of credit to you. You get a shiny new card in the mail and swipe it when you want to buy something. At the end of the month, you get a bill and pay the full balance, just like you would if you paid cash for all those things you bought. In return for paying for what you order, creditors and banks begin to trust you because you live within you means. *Seems simple enough, right?* Of course it does.

But what do so many people do instead? We get tempted by the ability to buy anything we want. We make minimum payments each month to stretch our budget, expose ourselves to exorbitantly high interest rates, and dig ourselves into a financial hole beyond comprehension – and it can take months, years, even *decades* to dig ourselves out.

At first glance, the convenience of minimum payments seems like a nice option. In reality, it's incredibly stupid. Think about it: if you went into Anthropologie and found that amazing new dress for $109, would you try to tell the unassuming employee working the register that you'll just make the minimum payment of $24 instead? That's essentially what you're doing when you make the minimum payment. And credit card companies are all too happy for you to do so, because it means they get to charge interest and make even more. The worse you are at managing your spending habits, the happier the credit card issuer is, because they get to make additional money on interest. All of a sudden, that $109 dress costs $140. It's great for them but not so great for you.

Types of Credit

There are two types of credit: secured and unsecured.

Secured credit is a loan that is backed by an underlying asset – the mortgage on your home, for instance. If you fall behind or default on your mortgage payments, the bank can foreclose on you, after which, they will own your home. In this case, your home is the "collateral" on the loan: if you stop paying, the bank has a backstop that "secures" the loan. Car payments also fit into this category.

Credit cards are considered *unsecured* credit – they're not backed by any underlying asset. There's no collateral. If you fall behind on your payments, you will accrue interest payments, but it's not like the bank can repossess your Anthropologie dress to collect their interest.

Some credit card debt can be "forgiven" in bankruptcy, but it depends on what type of bankruptcy you file. Chapter 7 bankruptcy allows the filer to walk away from debts entirely, and is often used by those whose debts are so high or income so low that after basic expenses they don't have the money for a payment plan. Chapter 13 bankruptcy allows the filer to draft a plan to repay all or part of the debts over three to five years. In other words, the bank won't repossess your house, but you will still have to pay based on an agreed upon schedule.

Why Credit Matters

As we've noted before, credit is necessary for many of life's big purchases. Some purchases, like a car or a home, usually can't be put on a credit card, but they are still bought on credit. Having a credit card can be a useful tool when you're in a bind and need money quickly. Using a credit card for life's everyday purchases can also be a convenient way to buy things and earn cash back, airline miles, or other perks in the process.

Essentially, your credit history tells lenders whether or not they can trust you to use the money responsibly. There are several factors that determine how "credit-worthy" you are to a lender.

Credit Reports: What You Need to Know

You're probably familiar with the concept of a credit report, but you may not know exactly what it is, how it's calculated, and why it matters so much. Put simply, your *credit score* is an indicator of your current financial "health" as it relates to credit, and your *credit report* is a comprehensive history of your (hopefully responsible) use of credit. Couching it in academic terms, your credit score is akin to a grade you receive in a class, and your credit report is the transcript that your school generates upon graduation, a fact pattern about how well or poorly you've performed.

Credit scores are measured on a scale of 300 – 850, with 300 being the worst score, and 850 the best (and hardest to attain). The numbers vary depending on whom you ask, but in general, a credit score between 300-579 is considered very poor credit, 580 - 619 is considered poor, 620 - 659 is fair, 660 - 699 is good, 700-759 is very good, and 760 - 850 is considered excellent.

760 - 850	Excellent
700 - 759	Very Good
660 - 699	Good
620 - 659	Fair
580 - 619	Poor
500 - 579	Very Poor

Your credit score is based on a variety of factors, each of which carry a different "weight" (i.e. some factors are more important to creditors than others). Consequently, each factor will affect your score in different ways. Below are some of the biggest factors that determine your credit score. Note that these percentages are approximations, and different credit reporting companies weigh the numbers differently:

- *Credit Card Utilization (accounts for around 35% of your total score): how much of your available credit you are actively using.*
- *Payment History (around 30%): how reliable are you in paying on time?*
- *Average Age of Credit (around 15%): how long have creditors trusted you? (Longer is better).*
- *Total Accounts (around 10%): how varied are your types of credit? (Having a car loan, a mortgage, and a credit card is theoretically better than having three credit cards).*
- *Credit Inquiries (around 10%): how many inquiries do you have on your report? (The fewer, the better).*

As an example of a credit report, here's a screenshot of the factors that are used to calculate my credit score, obtained from CreditKarma.com:

Take a look at your credit factors to see how you could improve.

Credit card use	Payment history	Derogatory marks
★★★ HIGH IMPACT	★★★ HIGH IMPACT	★★★ HIGH IMPACT
5%	**100%**	**0**
How much credit you're using compared to your total limits	Percentage of payments you've made on time	Collections, tax liens, bankruptcies or civil judgments on your report
view details →	view details →	view details →

Credit age	Total accounts	Hard inquiries
★★☆ MEDIUM IMPACT	★☆☆ LOW IMPACT	★☆☆ LOW IMPACT
3 YRS 2 MOS	**5**	**2**
Average age of your open accounts	Total open and closed accounts	Number of times you've applied for credit
view details →	view details →	view details →

As you can see, the highest impact factors are where it's most important to score well (utilization, payment history, and derogatory marks). My current utilization across my three credit cards is 5%, which is considered excellent. As a general rule, keeping your credit utilization under 9% earns the highest marks in this category.

Payment History is the second most important factor, and thanks to the magic of technology, I've never missed a payment in six years (*AutoPay is your friend*). One late payment can hurt you significantly: studies show that even having a 97% on-time payment history can substantially reduce your score.

My age of credit history is considered somewhat poor (since I'm only 26, this is fairly normal). When you're starting out, don't freak out if it says "very poor." Time is your friend, and it's not likely that you'll have a long credit history – that's ok. The only way to see a better score here is to wait. If you want to minimize the effects of having a poor score in this category, try not to open too many accounts. If you've got a card that works for you, stick with it. Don't open new cards unless absolutely necessary, and do *not* close old credit cards, even if you don't use them frequently. Keep one small monthly subscription on it and stick the card in your drawer. For instance, I keep a few random online subscriptions on my first credit card, which was a student credit card with almost zero perks to speak of. I hardly ever use it anymore – it's sitting in a drawer somewhere.

Why not cancel it? *Because it would take me a few years for my credit score to recover from the incomparably small convenience of not having a 1mm thick piece of plastic taking up space in my drawer.* You make the call.

I learned about Average Age of Credit the hard way. A few years ago I opened up two new cards in close succession (one business, one personal) in an attempt to spread spending across several cards and lower my utilization. This is usually a good tactic, but I forgot that I had my oldest credit card for over four years and opening accounts would cut in half my average length of credit. Age of Credit History is probably the single biggest factor that's holding me back from having a better score now, and it's totally my fault. My bad.

My Total Accounts is considered "poor," which came as a shock to me when I first looked at my credit score a few years ago. You may be in the same boat. After all, most twenty-some-things only have one credit card (if they have one at all). This ranking factor has improved over time as I acquired a mortgage (more on this later). I still don't have a car loan, so the four credit accounts I do have (3 credit cards and 1 mortgage) is still considered "poor." However, this category has a pretty low impact on my overall score, so there's no cause for real concern.

The last category is Credit Inquiries, which isn't a huge deal. Lots of people freak out about having a "hard inquiry" on their account. In reality, this is just fancy language for a lender looking at your report to see if you're worthy to extend credit. Just the fact that they looked will appear on your score, but if you only have one or two on your report, it's not a big deal – and they will drop off your report eventually.

Remember that seldom-used credit card that sits in my drawer? In an attempt to lower my utilization across all my cards, I called that credit card company and requested a credit limit increase from $500 (the initial limit from when I had opened the account six years ago) to $5,500. This was a quite reasonable figure for my income, but still a big jump (*an 1100% increase!*). The credit card company understandably is interested because they assume I'll carry a higher balance on my card and they'll get to profit from the 17% interest rate, or whatever it even is (I never even check - it doesn't matter to me, because I always pay in full monthly. They could charge 11,000% interest and I wouldn't lose sleep over it).

So they extend me the credit, assuming they will profit from my future poor financial choices. Little do they know that the only charge I'm going to put on that card is a measly $9.99 monthly subscription, which will account for a 0.18% utilization rate and is even *lower than my minimum monthly payment.* Imagine their disappointment. You can do the same.

However, doing so puts a "hard inquiry" on my report because they looked at my credit-worthiness. Whatever. It's my first hard inquiry, and it will drop off eventually.

So where does all that leave me? My current credit score is **767.**

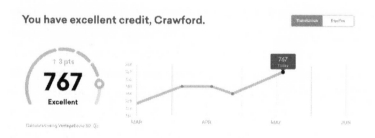

This isn't to pat myself on the back: there are plenty of people with even better scores than mine, most of whom have used credit responsibly for a longer period of time. I've made some mistakes along the way, and there are plenty of mistakes I could still make (but hopefully won't). If I continue to use my credit responsibly, make full payments, and manage balances, this score will improve over time, which means better interest rates on car loans, mortgages, and other credit cards.

Establishing credit from an early age and working to improve your score is very shrewd, especially when you don't need credit right away. When you do need credit in the future, you will be well-positioned to look as good as possible when it matters most. The longer you show yourself to be trustworthy to lenders, the more opportunities will open up to you.

Perks, Points, and Purchases: How to Make Credit Cards Work for You

Now that you understand the ins and outs of credit scores and what factors are most important in building good credit, let's get to the part that everyone loves to talk about: the perks.

If there's one thing that credit card companies understand, it's incentives. Credit card companies provide enticing incentives to sign up for their cards: points, airline miles, cash back, and many other rewards. Perks are one of the primary factors that influence our choice of credit cards, and up until now, they have been hugely profitable to the card issuers. According to the *Wall Street Journal,* "about 60% of American consumers are enrolled in a credit-card rewards program that offers benefits such as cash back on purchases, air-travel miles, points that can be redeemed for merchandise and other enticements."

Naturally, we'll go where the rewards are highest, and there is no shortage of credit cards that promise to cater to our every need. Fly a lot for work? There's likely a co-branded credit card for your favorite airline. Want cash back? There's a credit card for you. Shop a lot on Amazon? You guessed it: there's a card for that.

But with so many competing perks available to us, it can be hard to choose. Knowing what you know about credit scores and how they're calculated (too many cards is just as bad as too few), you need to be selective about "what's in your wallet." The best way to do this is to open an account conservatively. Much like an investor who's in it for the long haul, only open cards that you know you'll use and keep for a long time. For instance, I have three credit cards right now, and I plan on keeping them for the next 20 years.

Some people have rather curious practices regarding credit card use, but often it's not because they are stupid or have compulsive spending habits – they just don't know any better. For instance, I have a friend who's a destination wedding photographer. She does incredible work and charges premium prices for her services (her average wedding package *starts* at $8,000), but her credit card choices and habits surprised me. I don't know what she spends on her credit cards, nor do I need to know – it's none of my business. But when she told me that she frequently opens up new credit cards (mostly airline credit cards) to get the signup bonuses, getting her free flights whenever she needs to travel for a wedding, I knew she hadn't calculated the true cost.

To each her own I suppose, but to me her strategy seems "short-term smart, long-term stupid." For one, most cards only offer such rewards after you've hit a minimum spending require-ment. This can lead to unplanned, unnecessary spending. What's more, many airline credit cards carry an annual fee to provide these services, typically around $100/year or more. Most cards waive the fee for the first year, but it's always an unpleasant surprise when it kicks in 12 months later. This fee is how these card issuers subsidize their incentives, so don't expect to have any luck getting the fee waived. Think you can just cancel the card before the fee kicks in? We've already seen what that can do to your credit score and reputation, and how it can hurt you in the long run.

My friend's credit score would likely look much better if her choices were better informed. There can be benefits to signup bonuses and other teasers, but caution should always be exercised when opening up any new line of credit.

What's In My Wallet?

In the spirit of transparency, let's take a look in my wallet. I have three credit cards (four actually, but one of them sits in my drawer and earns me nothing, as we discussed previously). Two of these credit cards are American Express Delta SkyMiles cards (a Platinum personal card and a Gold business card). The other card, which my wife and I use most frequently is a Visa Chase Sapphire card.

I fly frequently on Delta, and have had a SkyMiles account for quite some time, so I acquired the Platinum Amex to begin earning miles with all my purchases. Combining a credit card with the miles I had already earned was a no-brainer, especially considering their 40,000 mile signup bonus at the time (last I checked, it's 50,000 miles). Before acquiring the other cards, this was my primary credit card. I'd use my debit card when a merchant wouldn't accept American Express, but I put everything else on this card.

I run my business as a sole proprietor, so I opened up the business Amex in the past few years. Doing so allowed me to separate business expenses from personal expenses (I waited far too long to do this), and it provided the extra bonus of earning another 40,000 miles after spending a certain amount on the card (which was well within my normal range of expenses). Getting a business card was a convenient way to separate expenses, but it was more strategic than that: business cards frequently have higher credit limits on them, and even though I'll never come close to using the available credit, it did wonders to drop my utilization percentage. Business expenses that were previously put on a personal credit card could now be (correctly) put on a business credit card, which dropped my utilization rate to only a few percent. My spending habits didn't change, but because I had good history lenders trusted me with more; as a result, what I continue to spend looks proportionally smaller because of the increased credit extended to me. Business credit cards make sense if you own a business or are a sole proprietor like me, but if that's not the case for you, don't be tempted to open one just to fix your utilization.

The Chase Sapphire card came after that, primarily because of a great 50,000 point signup bonus, double the miles on literally *all* travel and food purchases (fast food, restaurants, parking, Uber, flights – you name it), and one-to-one point transfer to several major airlines. As a rule, I'll use this card whenever I pay for anything food- or travel-related in order to maximize the points-earning potential. The one exception is if I am buying flights on Delta, since they offer double miles on purchases with their company. If both cards give me double points, I'd rather earn SkyMiles than go through the hassle of point transfers when I want to redeem points for free flights.

Of course, everyone's experience will vary when it comes to the perks and points that are right for them. A Delta credit card will be of no use to you if you never fly Delta, but a Chase Sapphire card might be of interest, since they have several partner airlines. And of course, if you don't fly a lot, you may want to consider a credit card with a generous cash-back program, or perhaps the Amazon Visa. As with every tactic we discuss in this book, your mileage may vary.

How to Be an Idiot

When it comes to credit cards, there are so many ways to make a mistake that it can be dizzying – and with the sheer volume of credit card advice out there, you're probably wondering: have I made any mistakes? Is there anything I could be doing better? When evaluating a topic such as how to build good credit card habits, it's often helpful to frame it in terms of what *not* to do. So let's take a look at some of the dumbest mistakes commonly made. If you can avoid the following mistakes, you'll be just fine.

MISTAKE #1: MAKING MINIMUM PAYMENTS

Minimum payments are one of the seemingly innocuous conveniences of a credit card, but if you want to stay in healthy financial condition, making a minimum payment is the equivalent of eating Tide Pods for breakfast. Make only the minimum payments and you'll rack up hundreds or even thousands of dollars in interest payments, digging yourself into such a deep financial hole that it may take years – even decades – to recover. Doesn't sound like fun? Didn't think so. The advice here is simple: pay off your credit card in full, every month. If you don't have the self control to pay the card off in full, don't get a credit card in the first place, or cut up the one you currently have.

MISTAKE #2: OVER-SPENDING

It may seem like the biggest no-brainer in the history of the universe, but if you don't want to get up to your eyeballs in credit card debt, don't ever spend more than you can afford. It's really that simple.

MISTAKE #3: NOT CHECKING YOUR CREDIT SCORE

While you don't need to be weirdly obsessive about your credit score to have a credit card, it's a good idea to take a look at your credit report once every few months. Credit reporting companies make mistakes from time to time, so if you find something that's odd, let them know. Checking your credit report is also a great way to spot identity theft. If you don't check, you won't know. If you're planning on making a big purchase in the near future (such as a car or a home), it's better to check your credit score more often to get a gauge on your score and make sure there aren't any unexpected surprises.

How Not to Be an Idiot

Now that we've covered how to be an idiot when it comes to credit cards, let's explore how *not* to be a idiot. The following items should routinely be monitored to keep your credit habits in check.

MINIMIZE YOUR FEES

As we've seen, most high-end credit cards with the appealing perks have yearly fees associated with them, sometime reaching into the multiple hundreds of dollars. Do your homework before opening up a new credit card: what are the fees? Are they waived for the first year? Will they ever increase?

Among my credit cards I pay around $300 per year in fees, but that's more than worth it for the benefits I derive from them. Just make sure the fees are worth it before you sign up…and if they're not, choose a different card that has better benefits or a smaller fee – or no fee at all. In the long run, you'll be thankful that you did.

MAXIMIZE YOUR REWARDS

While it's a good idea to have and utilize a credit card regardless of the perks it offers, taking a little extra time to select that first card can help you reap rewards where you didn't know there were any. For example, I got my first credit card in college. It was issued through my bank and was aimed at college students who had limited credit history – a good "starter card." It did offer points, but I would have had to spend thousands of dollars to redeem points for a measly $25 gift card. The points it offered just weren't worth it – they still aren't. But, like many other twenty-somethings just starting out, a credit card with no perks (used responsibly) is far better than no credit card at all. Since the point of the card was to build credit over time, I put a $10/month subscription on it and used AutoPay to build my credit. Rather than racking up a lot of credit card debt, I used my debit card or cash for most purchases.

Fast-forward a few years, and I had a steady job and some credit history, so I was ready to graduate to better cards with higher credit limits. After doing research, I got a Platinum Delta SkyMiles American Express, which carried a $195 yearly fee (waived for the first year). That's not an insignificant amount, but with their attractive 40,000 mile sign-up bonus, first checked bag free, and the number of miles I fly with Delta, the fee was more than worth it to receive free flights just for continuing in my everyday spending habits. I could have gone with a more inexpensive card, but the offers weren't worth it at the time. I received great perks (and still do) just because I did a little homework.

Homework is the name of the game: some cards offer frequent flyer miles, others offer cash back, rewards points, or membership perks at hotels. Some cards' benefits are better for balance transfers; others are better for students, frequent travelers, or relatively lower interest rates. It's up to you to decide which card is best for you and your current situation.

Fortunately, it's not hard – there are tons of great resources and reviews out there on the Internet for your consumption. For an in-depth list of the best cards for your financial situation, visit nerdwallet.com.

AUTOPAY IS YOUR FRIEND.

Without a doubt the most important piece of advice regarding credit cards is to use AutoPay. I don't know of a single credit card issuer who *doesn't* have AutoPay available through their website. Using AutoPay means that you don't have to worry about carrying a balance on your card, being hit with late fees, or seeing an unexpected drop in your credit score because of a late payment (which, as we've seen, can take a long time to recover from).

AutoPay is an extraordinary convenience, but only if you use it wisely. Be sure to have your AutoPay pay the *full* balance on your card (not the minimum payment) on the same day every month so that you're not hit with surprise bills.

Before You Move On

Before moving on to the next section, take some time to do the following:

- If you don't currently have a credit card, do at least one hour of research and apply for a card *before you read the next chapter.*
- If you already have a credit card (or multiple cards), go through this checklist to make sure you're using them wisely:
- **Check your credit report.** If you've never checked before, you can sign up for a free account at CreditKarma.com or similar sites.
- **Check your utilization.** If the balance on your credit card is above 9% of your credit limit, stop spending immediately and use your debit card (or cash) for everyday purchases until the balances are paid off in full. Then, set alerts on your credit card's website or mobile app to alert you when you're approaching 9% of your utilization. Many credit card issuers can send emails or text messages to alert you about your current balance.
- **Check your spending.** Is your spending within your monthly limits? If you need more help with this one, keep reading – we'll get to budgeting in Chapter Six.
- **Check your fees:** If you have fees associated with your credit cards, make those fees a line-item in your yearly budget so that you can be prepared for them.
- **Raise your limits.** As long as you haven't opened your credit card or requested an increase in the last 90

days, call your credit card company or visit their
website and request a modest credit limit increase.
Doing so will likely put a "pull" on your credit report,
and you may or may not get the increase you
request...but if your increase is granted, it will help
lower your utilization and promote a better credit
score.

———

ALREADY IN CREDIT CARD DEBT? We'll deal with this more in Chapter Seven, but for now, put all of your credit cards in a drawer and make paying off that debt a high priority. If you keep using your cards, you'll do more harm than good. If you want to be more protected against potential financial calamity, you need to have some money put aside – so next, we'll look at savings.

Chapter 3

LEARNING HOW TO SAVE

SURVIVING THE UNEXPECTED WITH ROOM
TO SPARE

S ociety tends to lump people into one of two categories when it comes to money: are you a saver or a spender? This often begins at an early age. When you're growing up, your parents may encourage you to save for things you want to buy, as mine did. But unless I had a tangible, audacious goal, I was prone to spend nearly ever dollar I earned as soon as I earned it. However, when I did have something to save for, I would go after it with reckless abandon. For instance, in high school I saved more than $4,000 for a high-end digital camera to help me do freelance photography (which more than paid for itself over the years).

It's easy to couch our habits and behaviors towards money in this type of language – *savers* and *spenders* – but often times, our disposition towards money is a bit more nuanced – it's not a binary thing. In some periods during our lifetimes we focus more on saving, while other times, we're a bit more spending-heavy.

However our habits may vary over the years and seasons of our lives, it's *the practice of learning how to save* that is of utmost importance. It goes back to the long-term mindset that we acquired in Chapter 1, and it's what we'll examine here.

Why Save at All?

"Why save?" It may seem like a profoundly dumb question, but an awareness of why we save in the first place can help us build better habits over time. By knowing our dispositions towards money, we can alter our behavior and build better financial habits in the future. Whether or not an old dog can learn new tricks is beyond me, but there's no better time than when you're young to learn how to save.

At a most basic level, there are so many things out there that we want to buy in the future – cars, homes, gadgets, experiences, vacations – you name it – and all of these things require money. There will always be more things that we want to buy that we do not have money for. If we want to acquire these items, we need to save.

Saving is not only practical, but also helps us develop healthy financial habits that prove beneficial in other areas of our lives, not just personal finance. As we've seen, one of those habits is delayed gratification, the act of consciously choosing to forego something today in an attempt to realize a greater future gain. Delayed gratification is at the heart of saving money, regardless of the motivation. By choosing to not spend money today, we will have more available to us later for large financial purposes, like rainy days, retirement, and the like.

Delayed gratification is not only an important mindset to adopt because it teaches us patience and leads to stronger willpower and self-control, but it has an obvious financial impact as well. Due to the forces of taxes and compounding, one dollar that you save right now is actually worth *more* than one dollar you spend right now. Think about it: every time you spend one dollar you could have invested, you don't just lose that dollar – you lose any future return you could have earned on it. When you adopt a long-term mindset and shift your focus towards investments and alternative uses for your money (something we'll explore in the next chapter), the opportunity cost of present spending is quite high.

And of course, in addition to all the items we plan to spend money on in our lifetimes, there are always the unexpected items as well: the proverbial rainy days. The emergencies. The unplanned expenses. No matter how much money you have in your bank account, things get messy from time to time. The unexpected happens (and usually at the worst time). It's inescapable, a fact of life.

Having money set aside to deal with these unplanned expenses is incredibly important throughout all seasons of your life. In our younger years, careers are still developing, salaries are low, and an unexpected event can set you back quite a bit. In the middle years, our expenses tend to rise: we have kids, buy houses, and have to worry about education and other items. Hopefully our salaries have increased, but there are just more obligations to spend money on. In retirement, when we're no longer working, we must live off the savings we have accumulated over the years. Failure to learn how to save early on has serious implications for us in the later stages of our life.

Setting money aside for large expenses – planned or unplanned – is a vital component of developing a healthy financial lifestyle. It's just one puzzle piece in a holistic view of wise financial management. According to a recent survey by the Federal Reserve Board, data suggests that 47% of Americans don't have $400 for an unplanned emergency expense *without borrowing money or having to sell something.* What's worse, nearly 1 in 5 Americans have exactly $0 set aside to cover unexpected emergency expenses.

An unplanned $400 expense isn't necessarily welcome news to anyone, but for nearly 1 out of 2 Americans, such an expense would put them in significant financial distress. And that's not all: according to a similar Bankrate survey performed in 2014, only 38% of Americans could cover a $1,000 emergency-room visit or a $500 car repair with money they had already saved and set aside. A Pew Research study indicated that 55% of American households didn't have enough liquid savings on hand to replace a month's worth of lost income. A job loss would likely spell financial disaster. What's worse, between 1970 and 2002 the probability that a working-age American would unexpectedly lose at least half her family income more than doubled. Times are changing. Clearly, we need to save.

Depending on your current financial situation, these statistics may either be incredibly astounding, or perhaps uninspiring altogether. Maybe a $400 car repair would put you in distress, or maybe you could cover it without needing to borrow money from friends or family. Regardless of your financial situation, it's a wise decision to always have more money set aside than you think you need. Life has a way of throwing expensive challenges at you when you least expect them – and certainly when they are least desired. Nobody wants to have to rely on friends or family to get them through tough times. It's up to you to prepare.

What's Behind the Anti-Savings Phenomenon?

Americans aren't particularly good at saving. This may not come as a surprise: perhaps you or someone you know has been personally affected by a lack of adequate savings to sustain them in an emergency or the loss of a job. If not, you've almost certainly heard stories about those who have.

Innate psychological influences beyond our control often govern how we treat money, and a number of societal shifts have occurred over the last century that may explain why we as a society are so bad at saving. There are a number of theories that seek to explain this phenomenon, some of which we'll examine here.

One of these theories asks if savings rates have declined because the poor and middle class went into significant debt to buy homes they couldn't afford. While periods like the 1990s were a great time for U.S. income growth, the personal savings rate fell by more than 5% while mortgage debt skyrocketed to an all-time high. This school of thought holds that many Americans gave up their saving habits in the turbulence of the 1970s, and by the time income growth finally caught up in the 1990s, many Americans had relied too heavily on credit to move into the suburbs, purchase cars, and accumulate other discretionary items. Thanks to a rise in mortgage debt, the real savings rate (i.e. the savings rate, adjusted for inflation) of the bottom 90% percent turned negative in 1998. We spend more than we have.

Another theory posits that U.S. policies make it easy for people to not save money. Thanks to government policies, retirement accounts such as 401(k)s are quite "leaky," which disincentivizes saving. As an example, for every $1 contributed to a 401(k), nearly 40 cents flow out from them due to premature withdrawals. Not only do these premature withdrawals hamper our ability to reap gains from the power of compounding, but they may be subject to additional taxes and penalties, which makes saving even harder. A lack of self-control with retirement accounts could explain part of the decline in saving rates, but it is more likely that a lack of self-control in other areas is to blame.

Perhaps the most convincing theory about the lack of savings in America revolves around conspicuous consumption. Theories about conspicuous consumption hold that America's mix of wealth and diversity is to blame: in a 2008 study, after controlling for income, it was found that minorities tend to save less than white Americans. It also found that even white people in poor states spent more of their income on "visible goods" – clothes, jewelry, watches, etc – than whites in higher income areas. Researchers claim that people of lower incomes, particularly in America, spend more on visible goods to signal to the rest of society that they're not poor.

The final theory we'll explore states that the pressure to keep up with richer neighbors has been fueled by rising income inequality. This theory hinges on what is called "trickle-down consumption": that households exposed to more spending by the rich report greater financial duress. It appears, then, that conspicuous displays of wealth are rather contagious. When people see their neighbors living the high-life, they are more likely to forego savings in an attempt to match their peers' consumption – the proverbial "keeping up with the Joneses" coming to fruition in real life. When fueled by rising income inequality that is so prevalent in our society, this may explain why personal savings rates are languishing.

This happens across all areas of the financial spectrum in America. When you see someone driving a sports car, you rarely think, " Wow, that person is cool." Instead, the thought that flashes through your mind is something more akin to, "If I had that car, people would think I'm cool." This is an interesting paradox of wealth that has profound effects on our savings and overall financial health: people want wealth to signal to others that they should be admired. But in reality, everyone is using your displays of wealth solely as a benchmark for their own desire to be admired.

All of these theories have elements of truth to them, and it is likely that no one theory can explain our lack of savings. However, when combined, all of these theories paint a bleak picture. We consume far more than is good for us, leveraging our lifestyles on credit that enables us to buy goods we can't really afford. Our bank accounts tell a sad story of lifestyles that reek of conspicuous consumption and poor self-discipline.

Combine these factors with a rising cost of living and many Americans feel they just can't afford to save. But while we cannot control external forces or when disaster strikes, our habit of self-discipline is something that we can control. It is futile to focus on what we can't control rather than what we can. Although it may seem like we can't afford to save, life will eventually teach us that we can't afford *not to*.

You Can't Expect the Unexpected...But You Can Plan for It

It's been said that the only two constants in life are death and taxes, but nearly everyone can think of unexpected circumstances that have caught us by surprise. A surprise illness, a fender-bender, or urgent home repairs like a burst pipe in the dead of winter or a broken air conditioner in the heat of summer can make us feel like we're drowning under the pressure of our financial obligations. We all know that these things can happen, so why don't we do a better job planning for them? Why do so few American adults have an emergency fund? Why don't people save more?

To address these questions, it's helpful to know a little bit about the psychology of risk and how the human brain works. The simple truth is that we don't like to think about unknown or ill-defined, nebulous possibilities. Psychologists have shown that we have a hard time imagining our *future selves* – given the way our brains work, it's incredibly difficult to adopt a long-term view. We have enough challenge just getting through the day.

It's much like the way people don't like to think about death, especially their own. Although we know such events are inevitable, it causes unnecessary anxiety, so we don't think about it. If we spent all our time worrying about everything that could possibly happen to us, we'd never get anything done. We literally wouldn't have the capacity to eat, sleep, or maintain relationships.

Psychologist Daniel Kahneman has done some incredible work in the field of decision science. In fact, his work won him a Nobel Prize for the contributions to behavioral economics he made along with fellow researcher Amos Tversky. Kahneman's research on the way humans make decisions is important because it gives us an accurate picture of how we assess risk.

Explained in his book *Thinking, Fast and Slow*, Kahneman argues that humans have a tendency to overestimate negative events that have a small likelihood of taking place, such as the probability that your home will burn to the ground (a 1 in 3000 chance). Conversely, we tend to underestimate negative events that have moderate to high probabilities of occurring, like the probability that you will get seriously injured in a car accident and accrue expensive medical bills that insurance may not entirely cover (a 1 in 114 chance).

Large losses cater to fear of the unknown – *I definitely wouldn't want to suffer the catastrophic loss of my home to fire, so I will purchase adequate insurance.* However, losses that are smaller in nature (having medical bills from being in a car accident) but have a much higher probability of taking place don't scare us as much. Therefore, we tend to underestimate the likelihood of their taking place and we (fail to) plan accordingly. We purchase expensive insurance for events that are highly unlikely to occur, but we fail to set aside a few thousand dollars for more minor expenses that are far more likely to occur.

Don't get me wrong: insurance exists for a reason, and having adequate insurance for things like your home is often a wise financial choice. But the fact that we spend money on insurance for very unlikely events while simultaneously failing to plan for events that are more likely to occur just isn't wise.

There's nothing like the fear of the unknown. In fact, it's one of the most powerful motivators there is. We would rather know with certainty a piece of terrible news than to be forced to wrestle with the unknown and the ambiguous. But if we are to be wise stewards of our finances, wouldn't it stand to reason that we should be actively preparing for the worst-case scenario, like a large expense or a period of prolonged unemployment? You would think so, but so few people do.

Instead, we leave things up to chance and make a conscious decision to not think about these unpleasant things. So we shirk our responsibilities, choosing to mistakenly adopt an overly rosy mindset and belief about the world. We put off what we incorrectly perceive as the difficult work of planning for the unexpected, figuring "it won't happen to me..." But what do we do when that unexpected emergency room visit finally happens or our car breaks down? If we aren't adequately prepared for life's unexpected events, we can find ourselves in a dangerous place. That's why we all need a conservatively-invested Emergency Fund.

Why Have an Emergency Fund? Why Not Just Money in a Checking Account?

Aside from the unpleasantness of thinking about unexpected expenses, the most common objection to setting up an Emergency Fund is one of convenience: if faced with unexpected circumstances, why not just dip into savings or pay for something out of our checking account? It's a perfectly valid question to ask, but there are a few reasons why establishing a dedicated Emergency Fund is a good idea.

I. YOU CAN SPEND MORE THAN YOU HAD PLANNED FOR.

The benefit of using your usual checking account for unplanned expenses is convenience. The downside of using your usual checking account for unplanned expenses is convenience.

Quite simply, if you pay for unplanned expenses out of a checking account, it can be harder to make ends meet when it comes to *regular and necessary* expenses, like rent and car payments. You can also unintentionally spend more money than you had planned on. Because your checking account has so much regular activity occurring in it on a monthly basis, it's all too easy to let things get out of control.

Transactions get muddied when money is being withdrawn from an account meant for a different purpose. If you have the foresight to plan for unexpected circumstances, it's best to have an account specifically designated for unplanned expenses, and only unplanned expenses. That way, you'll have a better handle on how much is in your emergency fund and how it's been growing over time.

2. If your money is sitting in a checking account, it's not working for you.

Most of us have checking accounts – it's where we pay for everyday expenses like food and rent. But if you're intentionally setting money aside for the unexpected, you don't just want it sitting there. For everyday expenses, you need a checking account that provides you immediate liquidity and stability. The expenses are so regular that you wouldn't want to risk your balance by seeking growth if the balance might be reduced as a result of the risk.

Unexpected expenses have a much different nature to them than everyday purchases. Because they occur much less frequently, you have a bit more leverage with those funds, more of a chance to allow them to grow. For example, I have an Emergency Fund, but it's not with a traditional bank account like Chase or Wells Fargo. I have a specifically-designated Emergency Fund in Betterment (a popular "robo-advisor"), and the money in that account is split 60%-40% between investments in stocks and bonds.

Investing money that's set aside for emergencies may seem overly risky, but if done carefully it's a terrific idea. While such a strategy involves more "risk" than setting money aside in a traditional checking or savings account, a conservative investment account provides the necessary liquidity, while at the same time leaving you some room for upside – a chance to grow your assets in that account over time. By placing my money in a designated Emergency Fund with a conservative allocation (more on this later), I can reasonably ensure that my money will grow over time, and I will reap the benefits of compounding. Hopefully I won't need to dip into this emergency fund often, if at all, and my investment will steadily grow over time. However, if I do need to access extra cash for an emergency, I can put emergency expenses on my credit card and transfer money reasonably quickly to cover the balance.

There is a chance that the stock market could experience a downturn and some of my money could "disappear" if I withdrew it – when you invest in anything, the possibility of loss always exists. This is why I have a mostly even split between investments in stocks and bonds – my allocation is fairly conservative. Many investment advisors would suggest a more conservative allocation (something like 70% bonds, 30% stocks), but it's a matter of preference. I'm still young and my expenses are fairly low, so I'm comfortable with this level of risk. In my case, the benefits outweigh the costs, especially if I have a balance large enough to cover more than my anticipated need in an emergency. Of course, everyone's situation is different and your situation is unique – you should begin with a risk assessment and determine the level of risk with which you are comfortable (and of course, consult a financial advisor if you're still unsure).

This brings us to the golden question of savings and emergency funds: how much do you need?

How Much Should You Save?

Perhaps the most controversial topic among financial advisors is how much you should actually have saved in an emergency fund. While it's easier to determine the amount of money we'll need for fixed expenses and aspirational purchases (a new car, a home, etc), unexpected circumstances and their accompanying price tags can vary quite dramatically.

A good idea is to begin by thinking about all the things that could go wrong. This exercise may be uncomfortable, but it is important. What if you were laid off from your job and it took 6 months to find new employment? What if that new job, seemingly the only one you could find, came at a substantial pay cut and wasn't enough to match current monthly expenses? What if you got in an accident and needed to repair (or worse, replace) your car? How much would any of those items cost? What if all of them happened at the same time? Would you be prepared? These questions aren't hard to answer but they aren't comfortable to contemplate. Unfortunately, if you want to be prepared for the unexpected, you have to address the uncomfortable.

I've found that when you're choosing to adopt a conservative approach to money by establishing an emergency fund in the first place, the best practice is to be as liberal as possible with your estimates and assumptions. In order to be adequately prepared, start by assuming the worst. As we've seen from Daniel Kahneman's research, we tend to overestimate the possibility of incredibly improbable events – but the financial cost of such events is not directly correlated with their probability. Although such events are very unlikely to occur, the financial burdens they impose are very real and are not mitigated by the fact that these events are highly improbable. So we must plan accordingly.

Conventional wisdom on this subject holds that your emergency fund should contain a minimum of three to six months of expenses. More liberal estimates (or conservative, depending on how you define it) say that your should have a minimum of six months worth of income in your fund.

These guidelines sound good, but how do people measure up? According to a 2016 survey by GOBankingRates, 69% of all Americans had less than $1,000 in a savings account. What's more, 34% of the people surveyed had zero savings at all. Here's a graph to explain how much money most Americans have set aside for emergencies:

As of February 2018, the median household income in America is $59,055, about $4,921 per month. Let's make a few assumptions and examine a single-income household earning the median national wage. This hypothetical household has been responsible: they have no credit card debt, and monthly expenses are equal to their income. They're not going into debt to finance their lifestyle, but they're also not getting ahead much, either.

Financial experts would recommend that this household have

six months of expenses saved to help buffet against unexpected circumstances. According to those recommendations, this family should have $29,527 saved. That may seem overly ambitious, a crazy high amount for an average earner. What if we take a more lax approach? Assuming we stick to the 3 months' expenses rule, this household would still need to have saved $14,764.

And yet, how much are they likely to have saved? According to the statistics, only 15% of Americans have saved more than $10,000. Even the most conservative saving goal (1 month's worth of expenses) would put them at $4,900. Only 11% of Americans have saved close to that much.

With no savings to speak of, an emergency room visit or loss of a job could put their finances in peril. Even with $5,000 set aside (not a paltry sum of money), a month-long job search would wipe out their savings and put them in serious financial jeopardy. Grouping the respondents by age group helps us see a more accurate, albeit still bleak, picture:

These statistics are sobering to say the least. Assuming a median wage, only 2 in 10 Millennials have enough money saved for the commonly-held "three to six months' expenses" rule. The other 8 out of 10 will be in a financial bind, forced to rely on credit, friends, or family. This isn't necessarily surprising for Millennials with fairly low wages and lots of student debt, but it doesn't get better as we age: 37% of older Gen-X adults have $0 set aside, while only 31% of Millennials do. This near-zero savings rate doesn't seem to change much over the course of our lifetimes, either: 62% of seniors over the age of 65 have less than $1,000 in savings.

No wonder our society has such a credit problem: we rely on credit to live beyond our means, which depresses savings rates to near-zero...and when the proverbial rainy day comes, we're forced to add to our debts just to sustain ourselves. It's a vicious downward spiral. These numbers and statistics paint a picture of "doom and gloom." If your savings account isn't there yet, you now possess the knowledge you need to set yourself up for success and to formulate a plan to begin saving.

With investment tools like Betterment you can set up an Emergency Fund quickly, using tools like auto-deposit so that a certain amount of money is deposited every month. If you can't cover three months of expenses yet or don't have a big chunk of money to set aside all at once, break your deposits into smaller amounts and make them regularly, perhaps with each paycheck. By placing your money into a conservatively-allocated investment account, you'll benefit from positive market changes and, with any luck, see your fund grow over time.

My Emergency Fund is Funded. Now What?

So, you've done the work: you've diligently set aside some money every few weeks and are watching your Emergency Fund grow slowly and steadily. Maybe you're working towards one, three, or six months' worth of expenses. Maybe you've already reached your desired level. What to do now?

The best thing you can do...is nothing.

Seriously. Just let your money sit there. It may seem anti-climactic, but an Emergency Fund is designed for just that: a true emergency (not a vacation). Even if your account is already fully-funded, you may want to keep making regular contributions as you are able to give yourself a bit more of a buffer. Having an Emergency Fund takes self-discipline – don't withdraw or move the money unless absolutely necessary for an emergency. If your monthly expenses or living situation changes, adjust your contributions accordingly.

As you get older or your financial situation changes, you may need to adjust your allocation or the size of your fund. Hopefully your Emergency Fund will grow and you won't need to make any withdrawals, but as you age and your financial situation changes, you may want to consider a more conservative allocation, favoring bonds over stocks. Reevaluate your Emergency Fund at least once per year to make sure it's in line with your financial needs. If your income or monthly expenses change, ensure that your emergency fund can still cover several months' worth of expenses. Tools like Betterment and other popular investment services can help you do so. Just be sure to check in occasionally to get a temperature on your fund's progress and make sure everything is in order.

Before You Move On

Now that you understand emergency funds better, it's time for some homework. You'll fall into one of three categories:

You don't (yet) have an Emergency Fund.

Before you move on, open up an account with an investment service like Betterment (sign up here and get 90 days managed free). They have some great tools to help you reach your financial goals faster, you won't pay commissions on the money you invest, and their management fee is very inexpensive.

Set up an Emergency Fund in Betterment and fund it, beginning with an auto-deposit on a regular schedule. This amount can be small at first (contribute as you are able), but be sure to get into the habit of contributing to it at least once a month. As we've said before, it's less about the amount and more about getting into the right habits.

You have an Emergency Fund, but it's not quite big enough yet.

You have an Emergency Fund – great! You're more than halfway there. If it's not quite funded to the level that you feel comfortable, take some time to assess your finances and see how much you can contribute on a regular basis. After accounting for your daily needs and non-negotiable expenses, try to contribute as much as you possibly can to fund it. Not only will this provide you with a cushion sooner rather than later should disaster strike, but as we've seen, the power of compound interest shows that you'll earn more money over time the sooner you put it in – so keep contributing!

Your Emergency Fund is fully funded.

This is where you want to be: your emergency fund is set up and can fully cover all expenses for a prolonged period of time. If you are able, try to keep contributing a regular amount every month (it could only be $100) so that you can take advantage of market moves and continue to watch your money grow over time.

———

IN OUR NEXT CHAPTER, we'll go beyond the basics of a conservative Emergency Fund and learn how to invest in the stock market to watch our wealth *really* grow over time.

Chapter 4

THE FUNDAMENTALS OF INVESTING

EVEN WARREN BUFFET STARTED SOMEWHERE

W e've learned a lot about personal finance up to now: the value of time, the inner workings of credit, and the importance of saving for the unexpected and for the future. Now if you want to get ahead financially and build a nest egg for yourself over the long term, this is where the rubber meets the road: investing.

Investing is one of the most common topics of personal finance. Often glorified in movies like *The Wolf of Wall Street*, it's hard for us for divert our attention elsewhere when the topic of investing comes up. We're excited by the prospects of striking it rich, eager to day trade our way to a million dollars – or more.

But for all the hype, proper investment strategy is often the least understood and most feared aspect of finance, especially among Millennials and twenty-somethings. In a 2015 survey by Capital One ShareBuilder, 93% of Millennials say that both distrust of financial markets and lack of investing knowledge make them less confident about investing. Nearly 60% of Millennials surveyed say they do not trust financial markets, and three in five Millennials lack any exposure to the stock market. This is most likely due to the stresses imposed by the Great Recession that began in 2008, where the financial resources of millions of Millennials and their families were largely wiped out. As a result, young Americans are not embracing the stock market in the same way that has helped previous generations accumulate wealth.

Due to the effects of compounding over time, this phenomenon has serious implications for the financial health of younger generations. If we're not actively saving and participating in financial markets, we can't reap the rewards they offer. Combine this with the fact that 40% of Millennials plan to fund at least a portion of their retirement with Social Security benefits (an expectation that may not pan out), and we find ourselves in trouble. According to a NerdWallet analysis of federal data, most Millennials in the class of 2015 (my college graduation year) won't be able to retire until we're 75. The post-crisis hangover is real, and it's not pretty.

What can be done? If we don't want to be caught without resources at retirement age, it is imperative that we begin to invest a portion of our earnings in financial markets immediately.

But isn't it risky? That's one of the most common concerns many younger people have about the prudence of investing at such an early age. At a time in our lives when our earning power is fairly low but expenses like student debt repayment and moving expenses seem to eat up more than their fair share of our paychecks, a bit of wariness is certainly understandable. So let's begin with a word about risk and opportunity.

Understanding Risk

It's not necessarily *risk* that stops Millennials from investing – it's uncertainties surrounding risk and which particular investment activities are actually risky ventures that prevent us from taking action.

Investing seems risky. After all, why on earth would we engage in unnecessary risk with our hard-earned money when we're young and life is expensive? These are valid questions. Chances are you have student debt, or maybe you haven't made the wisest choices with your credit cards during and after college. Perhaps you just graduated and moved to a new city where living is expensive, incurring moving costs along the way. Or maybe your unreliable beater of a car just broke down and you need a new way to get around.

Life is expensive for many who are just starting out. It may feel like you can't dig out from the financial hole that student debt, credit cards, and life's situational factors have thrust upon you...and that's ok. If meeting your real needs on a monthly basis is an actual struggle, you don't have to begin investing yet – but you should start learning now.

Once you're able to meet your monthly needs, set some money aside for a rainy day and still have a bit left over, investing in the stock market is one of the smartest ways you can put your money to use. It may seem scary – *what if I lost it all?* – but in reality, investing is one of the least risky decisions you can make at your age. Why? Because when there isn't much money to invest, there isn't much money to lose. What's more, you may not have a spouse, kids, or a mortgage to pay either, and if you lose in the short-term, you have a lot of time to make it up, so it all averages out.

It goes back to the story of a baby in diapers learning to walk for the first time. When they first try to walk, they're going to fall – a lot. And so will you. Graduating college, getting your first real job, or moving to a new city are all huge opportunities that may come with their fair share of stumbles and failures. But when there's comparatively so little on the table, even the effect of the worst mistake you can imagine is negligible in the grand scheme of things.

Investing is no different, and that's why you should begin an investing habit now. Suppose you lose a few hundred dollars on a bad trade. What's the worst that can happen? You go into foreclosure on your home, declare bankruptcy, and have to auction off every asset you own? Not even close. You're young: you don't have a house, your only real asset is probably your car, and you can even move back in with your parents if the going gets really tough. It's not ideal, but it's not the end of the world, either.

Investing 101: It's Not About the Money

If there's one thing I wish I could teach every twenty-something about investments, it's that *it's not about the money*. We've explored this concept before: the most valuable asset you have is not the balance of your bank or investments accounts, but rather time and the knowledge and habits that you have developed by starting your own personal financial journey from an early age. The dollar amounts don't matter as much as the mindset; your balance isn't as important as your habits. The end goal is insignificant compared to the process at this stage of your life.

If you listen to popular financial personalities, in time you'll come to believe that investing is all about picking the next hot stock or timing the market right so that you strike it rich overnight. This could not be further from the truth. In reality, it's incredibly hard – impossible, actually – to time the market or come up with a formula for picking the next Facebook or Google. And yet so many investors, from the experienced to the novice, try to do just this.

If you want to be a successful investor, don't focus on returns – focus on the process. Investing is about patience, and patience is a habit that takes time to form. It doesn't matter if you have a billion dollars to invest: if you're impatient, you'll likely make a terrible investor. I'd rather be a patient twenty-something with $1,000 to invest than an impatient 40-year-old with $100,000. If you have patience and discipline, chances are that you will perform better in the long run.

Remember, You're Already a Millionaire

By now, you know that time is the most valuable asset you have at your disposal, and you have a lot of it. That's the most important thing to keep in mind when you start investing at a young age. You're probably already sick of me saying it, but *time is your friend.* There's no way around it: you will be better off by learning how to invest – and starting now – even if you only have $100. By using the leverage of time and patient, consistent actions, you'll build more wealth than if you start ten years from now with ten times as much money.

Most people (especially those who are younger) believe one of two things about the stock market: either that you have to pick the next Google, or that you have to already be mega-wealthy and invest huge sums into the stock market to make a decent return.

Both of these assumptions are false. Plenty of people have amassed fortunes in the markets – not by investing a lot to begin with, but by starting at an early age and consistently buying equities over time. If you want to have a healthy portfolio that earns you good income and builds your nest egg over time, the best thing to do is to do it now.

So, are you a little nervous about investing? Good. You're not supposed to know what you're doing. You're not supposed to have a clue about where to start. There are three key elements to become a successful investor:

1. A willingness to learn.
2. Patience and consistency.
3. A long-term mindset.

Investing In Your Twenties: A Simple Guide

A disclaimer: I'm not a financial advisor, and I don't do this for a living. I have my limitations. There are plenty of people out there who have far more knowledge than I do about investing, so we're going to take a page out of their book to learn about investments. And who better to listen to than Warren Buffett, the "Oracle of Omaha"?

Warren Buffet has a remarkable story. Growing up as the second of three children in Omaha, Nebraska, he lived out his childhood years in a relatively modest way. He displayed an interest in business at an early age, often times engaging in different entrepreneurial ventures as a youngster, from door-to-door sales to buying pinball machines and leasing them to local businesses. As he grew up, he eventually graduated from buying and selling pinball machines and Coca-Cola bottles to buying and selling significant stakes in entire companies...*like Coca-Cola, for instance.*

Over the years, Buffett has proven himself with impressive annual returns on investment, and has been hailed by many as one of the most successful investors of all time. With a net worth of $83.6 billion , he's shown that he knows a thing or two about investments. That's why investors the world over – from hedge fund managers and fellow billionaires to young, aspiring investors like you and me – tend to listen when he speaks.

So what does the Oracle of Omaha have to say about investments? Not surprisingly, he has a lot of wisdom to share. Here are some of the highlights:

On risk: *"Risk comes from not knowing what you are doing."*

On long-term investing: *"Only buy something that you'd be perfectly happy to hold if the market shut down for ten years. If you aren't willing to own a stock for ten years, don't even think about owning it for ten minutes."*

On patience: *"Someone's sitting in the shade today because someone planted a tree a long time ago."*

On discernment: *"The difference between successful people and really successful people is that really successful people say no to almost everything."*

Again, on patience (one of my favorites): *"Successful investing takes time, discipline, and patience. No matter how great the talent or effort, some things just take time: You can't*

*produce a baby in one month by getting nine women
pregnant."*

Buffett is a proverbial fountain of wisdom when it comes to
investments and financial markets. These quotes are just sound-
bytes, conveniently lifted and taken out of context, but there are
a few common themes underpinning all of them: patience, discipline, and a willingness to go against the flow.

These are themes we've explored thus far. But what about the
practical, tangible applications of these themes? If an average
person was given $10,000 to invest, what would Buffett advise
him or her to invest it in? Probably just one thing: *low-cost index
funds.*

Index Funds 101

First, an explanation: what is an index fund? An index fund is a
type of fund that tracks a representative quantity of securities in a
market index (for example, all stocks in the S&P 500) in a way
that replicates the performance of the index itself. Put simply, it's
a relatively easy way of matching the return of the overall stock
market (or a portion of it). Rather than buying individual stocks
like Apple or Coca-Cola, an index fund lets your returns match
the returns of the entire stock market. If the S&P 500 was up
8.2% last year and your portfolio was comprised of an S&P 500
index fund, guess what? You grew your money by 8.2% as well.

Index funds have a few distinct advantages over traditional
investments. For one, they are very low-cost ways to invest your
money. In a traditional exchange-traded fund (ETF), fund
managers on Wall Street make their money from management
fees. Every fee they impose eats away your earnings: the higher

their fees, the lower your return. If you have money in their fund, you're paying them to manage it for you, which means that you walk away with less, regardless of their performance. This is often a bad thing, not only because you have to pay significant fees to park your money in such a fund, but also because the ADHD-like tendencies of Wall Street fund managers means that returns can quickly be wiped out by overactive investing behavior. *Remember Buffett's advice about being willing to own an asset for ten years?* Good luck finding that with a traditional Wall Street fund manager.

In contrast, index funds are passively-managed by computer algorithms, meaning that the returns of the index fund will always closely match the returns of the overall market index they're tracking. Because there's less overhead of employing managers and people to do the work that computers do for them, index funds are able to charge much more modest fees, usually from 0.05% to 0.25%. Put $10,000 in, and you'll end up paying between $5 to $25 per year to watch you money grow. Compare that with a common 1% fee that fund managers charge ($100 on a $10,000 account), and you'll quickly realize that extra $75 to $95 is better off in your pocket than in the pocket of some rich guy on Wall Street. Some fund managers charge a 2% fee if your account balance is low, like under $100,000. Over the long-term, low-cost index funds are typically upper second-quartile perform-ers, meaning that they perform better than 65-75% of actively managed funds. Also, most index funds pay dividends, so you can reinvest this (essentially free) money and build your wealth dramatically over time. Remember what we said about the power of compounding money over time? Index funds fit the bill.

The Returns of Asset Types Over Time

Knowing what we know about conventional wisdom (trying to "time" the market or finding the next hot stock) and the investments Warren Buffett has made (he buys and sells entire companies, after all), his strategy may seem counter-intuitive. Why buy an index fund that tracks the returns of the market? Don't the most "successful" investors trade in and out of positions all the time and even make large acquisitions? Well yes, that happens quite regularly. But if you're not a hedge fund manager, active trading and making outsized bets on individual equities aren't wise strategies.

So what about investments in other assets, such as bonds, gold, or cash? Looking at the historical averages of American markets over the past 200 years, we see an interesting phenomenon as it relates to the returns all common assets provide and the overall wealth-building capacities of each:

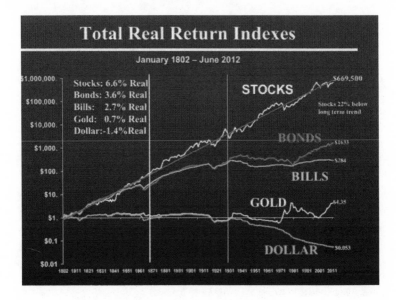

This chart shows how much purchasing power you'd have in 2012 if you had invested $1 in each of these assets back in 1802 (importantly, this chart is in *real* terms, meaning it's adjusted for inflation and the rising cost of living over time).

Let's begin with **stocks**, one of the most common investments. Investing $1 in 1802 would give you $669,500 at the end of 2012. Keep in mind, this means your investment was $1 total – you never contributed any additional money, and you let dividends reinvest over time. These numbers give stocks a long-term return of 6.6% per year.

What about **bonds**? Bonds are a common investment, and while their return is good, it's not nearly as much as stocks. The real return of bonds is 3.6%. That doesn't seem too different than stocks – an extra 3% per year couldn't matter that much, could it? Turns out it does: an extra 3% per year adds up to an extra $667,867 over time.

Bills (another word for short-term government bonds) are another popular investment choice, but their returns aren't nearly as good. A $1 investment in government bills in 1802 would only give you $284 today, a 2.7% return.

What about **gold**? It's seen as a symbol of wealth, but how much does it appreciate over time? As it turns out, not much: a $1 investment 200 years ago would only be worth $4.35 today.

And finally, what about the almighty **dollar**? It may be the closest thing our world has to a universal currency today, but its return as an investment isn't just worthless, it's worse: thanks to inflation, a $1 investment way back when would give you a nickel today, a −1.4% real return each year for 200 years.

When you patiently adopt a long-term mindset, stocks are the clear winner for building wealth most efficiently. As Aristotle once said, "Patience is bitter, but its fruit is sweet." There's simply nothing like the stock market for building massive amounts of wealth over time.

And yet, most Americans don't understand. They see the stock market as excessively risky and favor cash in the bank instead. But that strategy isn't working for them. I suspect that if more people were exposed to this graph, they'd understand the true value of their dollars – or more accurately, the true value of their dollars depending on where their dollars reside.

"But What If...?"

What if the market tanks? Won't I lose all my money?

There is always a chance that the market won't do as expected. Take the first half of 2016 for example, when all markets were down nearly 15% in the first 6 months of the year. Not exactly what everybody had hoped for.

Conversely, the market can react in ways that are counter to popular opinion, yet very beneficial. Just look at the election of Donald Trump to the U.S. Presidency in 2016. The markets were showing significant turbulence on pre-election worries, but after Trump won, the market rallied 11.6% during his first 100 days in office and continued to climb, resulting in a 26% gain during his first year in office. Markets fluctuate, but time has proven that investing in the stock market is a solid investment decision.

Yes, the market can always go down, but if you're smart about your investments, don't put all your assets in one place, and remain patient, you can see your net worth appreciate in a way that a traditional bank account can never do for you. The American market (and the economy in general) is incredibly resilient, and over time, will provide much better returns than you'd get anywhere else.

Listen to what Buffett has to say about the stock market:

"In the 20th century, the United States endured two world wars and other traumatic and expensive military conflicts; the Great Depression; a dozen or so recessions and financial panics; oil shocks, and the resignation of a disgraced president. Yet the Dow rose from 66 to 11,497."

That's a return of 17,320%. If you had the opportunity to put $100 into the markets in 1900, by 2000 you would have $17,320. Put $10,000 in (yes, that would have been a ton of money back then), and you'd end up with $1,732,000.

I've said it before, and I'll say it again: if you want to grow your net worth over time, there is nothing like the stock market to do it for you, and there is no time like the present to start.

How To Begin Investing

So if you're interested in investing with index funds, how can you actually do it? Well, it's pretty simple: find a broker, buy some index funds, and wait.

My favorite broker is Betterment. As mentioned earlier, Betterment is what's called a "robo-advisor," a financial advisor that is built upon a set of computer algorithms and requires minimal human intervention. While you could open up an account at a traditional investment brokerage, there are a few reasons I like Betterment, well, *better.*

First, Betterment charges a very low management fee. It depends on how much you have invested with them, but as of this writing, there is a 0.25% yearly fee on balances up to $100,000. The fee increases to 0.40% above $100,000, and comes with unlimited access to Certified Financial Planners and in-depth advice for investments outside of Betterment.

Second, Betterment lets you set up separate accounts within its service (such as a retirement account, an emergency fund, traditional and Roth IRAs, etc). Upon setting up a new account, you will have an opportunity to specify a time horizon and regular contributions, and Betterment will advise you on how to adjust your allocation of stocks and bonds, as well as how much you need to invest on a regular basis in order to reach your financial goals. It's like having a financial planner at your fingertips, but it's built upon software – and unlike many investment advisors, they don't charge any performance fees.

Third, Betterment allows for automatic reinvestment of dividends, so you can watch your account balance grow over time. Another great feature is what they call "Tax Loss Harvesting." Using this feature, when you withdraw funds, Betterment will automatically sell the worst-performing assets in order to offset any taxes you'll have to pay. Automatically minimizing your tax bill without any effort? Sign me up.

With Betterment, you can create "Tax-Coordinated Portfolios" that spread different asset types across different accounts, depending on their tax advantages. Utilizing this strategy, Betterment will direct tax-advantaged accounts like IRAs to hold securities that are highly taxed, while lower-taxed assets are held in taxable accounts. According to Betterment's research, this strategy can boost after-tax returns by an average of 0.48% per year, which amounts to approximately an extra 15% return over thirty years.

Fifth, creating and funding an account is incredibly easy. During account setup, you can direct Betterment to make automatic deposits on custom schedules (for instance, 10% of your paycheck every two weeks).

Finally, Betterment's portfolios allow you to invest in thousands of companies around the world. Their stock indexes track the total U.S. market, including small-, mid-, and large-cap companies, developed international markets, and emerging international markets. Their bond funds are comprised of U.S. inflation-protected bonds, high quality investment-grade U.S. corporate bonds, municipal bonds, international developed market bonds, and more.

Common Mistakes and How to Avoid Them

By now this investing thing seems easy, right? By and large, it is. But you'll need to know some of the most common mistakes young investors make in order to avoid them and come out ahead of the pack. The mistakes that young investors make can commonly fall into a few categories:

Mistake #1: Trading Too Actively

Too much activity in an investment account usually has negative consequences for the young investor. It seems glamorous in the movies: fast-talking traders screaming at each other, moving in and out of positions and causing a flurry of activity on the trading floor. But that's not actually how Wall Street works; plus, you want to be smarter than Wall Street.

A much better strategy for the young investor is to *buy and hold*. Seriously. It's that simple. Contribute money to investment accounts like Betterment, invest them where you see appropriate, and let them sit there. Your mindset should be like Warren Buffett's: if you wouldn't hold it for 10 years, don't hold it for 10 minutes. Remember, long-term mindset.

Wall Street Journal columnist Jason Zweig noted in an interview, "The default position of any investor should be to do nothing – it doesn't cost anything when you do nothing. As investors, we should trust our intuition and our gut when making investment decisions." And as Warren Buffett himself famously said, "Our investment philosophy borders on lethargy."

Mistake #2: Forgetting About Taxes

Another huge mistake is to not think about the tax consequences of your trading activity. We'll cover taxes more in the next chapter, but there are a few basic things you need to know. Although you won't incur commissions on trades performed in tools like Betterment, each trade you make creates a taxable event, which means that any money you have earned on your trades is lessened by the taxes you'll owe on the profitability. Every time you sell a financial asset, you'll incur taxes that are due every April. For investments that are held longer than a year, you'll incur what's called *long-term capital gains* taxes. The current tax rate for long-term capital gains (as of 2018) is 15% for most people, although your rate may be 0% if you earn less than $38,700 a year as a single person. The highest long-term capital gains rate is 20%, but you'd have to be earning more than $426,700 a year to pay that rate.

For investments held less than 365 days, you'll incur (you guessed it) *short-term capital gains taxes.* These rates are *much* higher than long-term capital gains taxes, which is a way the government incentivizes people to hold onto their investment for a longer term. Short-term capital gains are taxed as ordinary income, so you'll have to check and see which tax bracket you're in. For instance, if you earned the national median wage of approximately $55,000 in 2018, any investments you held for less than a year and sold would get taxed at a rate of 22%. If you sold after holding onto investments for more than a year, you'd be taxed at a rate of 15%. In almost all cases, short-term capital gains are taxed at a higher rate than long-term capital gains. That's a strange feature of our tax code (but one that you can use to your advantage): in America, "unearned" income (income derived from investments) is actually taxed *less* than "earned" income (income earned from productive labor).

Mistake #3: Investing Too Much

This may seem counterintuitive. Isn't this chapter about being wise with your money and growing wealth over time by investing it? Well, yes, but it's not smart to invest too much. Investing is important, but you should focus on eliminating debt first, covering monthly expenses, and building a robust emergency fund. Before you have done these things, it's not very wise to invest, because you don't have as much of a margin for error in your daily living.

Think about it this way: imagine you couldn't withdraw any money you've put into your investment accounts for at least 20 years, would you still deposit that money? If the answer is yes, then go ahead and invest. If that thought makes you uncomfortable, consider investing a smaller amount, working your way up to larger amounts as you feel comfortable.

MISTAKE #4: NOT HAVING A PLAN

Investing without first sitting down to think about your goals is foolish. Are you looking to save for retirement? Minimize taxes with your investments? Establish a conservative emergency fund? What's your time horizon? Are you seeking to preserve capital or to derive income from your investments? Looking to save for college or a down-payment on a house? Without a clear plan in mind, it's too easy to change your mind and see your earnings take a hit as a result. But with a plan, you'll know how to invest, what to invest in, and when to take money out.

MISTAKE #5: NOT REBALANCING

Rebalancing is an essential component of investing. Rebalancing is the act of taking a look at what you're invested in and adjusting your investments to make sure that they're still achieving your desired outcome. Too heavily invested in stocks?

It might be time to buy some more bonds. Too many tech companies in your portfolio? Maybe it's time to buy some more utilities or financial sector equities.

While the act of rebalancing is aimed primarily at those who invest in individual companies, it still does apply to those who are heavily invested in index funds. Luckily, Betterment's algorithms do this for you, so you won't have to actively manage your account.

One thing to keep in mind is that because stocks are typically more "risky" than bonds, you need to have the correct mix of stocks and bonds. When you're younger, this may look like a portfolio comprised of 90% stocks and 10% bonds, but as you get older and take on more financial obligations (kids, a mortgage, etc), it would be devastating if your portfolio dried up and you didn't have anything to lean back on. The general rule of thumb when determining asset allocation is to subtract your age from 100 – that's the percentage of equities (stocks) you should hold in your portfolio. As you age, you should gradually decrease your exposure to stocks over time, favoring bonds and more conservative investments instead, which will reduce risk and provide the additional cash flow needed as you approach retirement.

Imagine retirees like your grandparents: if they were invested in 90% stocks and there was another credit crisis like the Great Recession of 2008, they could see their life savings dry up in an instant. But if they had appropriately rebalanced over time, their portfolio would likely be 90% bonds and 10% stocks. It may still take a hit, but at their age, that's a much more appropriate and balanced portfolio.

Mistake #6: Getting Emotional

Emotional decision-making is the cardinal sin of investments, and one that younger investors are especially susceptible to. There's a reason that car rental companies charge a premium to rent to people under the age of 25: at that age, the frontal lobe of the brain hasn't fully developed yet, which means we're particularly vulnerable to acting with emotions instead of letting level-headed decision-making dictate our behavior.

The same risk is true when it comes to investing: we see money start to dry up or hear news of a "market correction" in the media, and we panic. We instantly sell off our assets, thinking that we are more "safe" if we have money in our pockets and out of the market. That's not wise. But time and time again, young inexperienced investors fall prey to emotional stories and quickly lose money that they can never recapture. Learning to approach the market with discernment is something that takes patience and practice. It's a skill only learned over time, and sometimes it takes drastic outcomes to avoid being too emotional.

I'll give you an example. A few years ago, I had a sizable chunk of my assets invested in the stock market. They were appropriately balanced and adjusted for risk, but the market can still do crazy things. For instance, one day the market declined sharply and shed several percentage points in a single day. People were worried about the Fed raising interest rates, a nuclear test in North Korea, and the price of oil was taking a big hit. In a matter of a few hours, I "lost" nearly $800 on paper. Actually, that's not quite true. I didn't lose anything because I didn't sell. But it sure didn't feel good.

Nobody likes hearing bad news. Nobody likes watching hundreds of dollars "disappear" from their lives. Nobody likes being told that an investment they made didn't pan out the way they were expecting. It's just not fun.

In my head, I knew that I didn't really lose any money. I knew that the market would rebound eventually (which it did), though it took some time. But my heart was telling me something else. It was fearful in the moment, telling me that I should sell everything and get out completely. Those rumors of a market correction came from smart people, after all.

There's a chance the Fed could raise rates and the market could dry up.

Would it cause another recession?

Would 2016, the year I really started investing seriously, become one of the worst years in recent memory?

When I took the time to remember my long-term strategy, I didn't care about daily fluctuations. I was invested for the long-haul, so even if I "lost" money then, it didn't really matter – I wasn't going to be withdrawing it any time soon anyway.

So what did I do when I heard the news? I knew that if I looked at my investments too closely, I'd be susceptible to making rash and emotional decisions, so I deleted my finance apps from my phone. I couldn't control what was happening in the markets, but I could limit my access to the doom and gloom. So I cut off my access to the investment apps that would have allowed me to make hasty and foolish decisions.

Before You Move On

Before you move on to the next chapter, assess where you stand with investments.

1. Are you able to meet your monthly expenses? Have you paid off your debt? If the answer to both of these questions is yes, move on to #2.
2. Have you established an emergency fund, and is it funded to a satisfactory amount? If so, move on to #3.
3. Open an account with Betterment or another advisor of your choosing. Pick an allocation that is appropriate for your goals, fund your account, and most importantly, set up automatic deposits so that your balance will grow over time.

———

Now that you've established an investment habit, it's time to address one of the most common "gripes" many people have about personal finance (and incidentally, one of the least-understood among younger people like us): taxes.

PART II

OUR PROBLEMS
WITH MONEY

Chapter 5

EVERYBODY LOVES TAXES

YOU KNOW WHAT THEY SAY...

I t has been said that only two things in life are inevitable: death and taxes. It's true: we all die, and unless you want to spend your life in federal prison for tax evasion, you're going to have to pay at some point.

April 15, tax day, is dreaded by most Americans. Complaining about taxes is nearly as universal as small talk about the weather. Nobody likes seeing part of their hard-earned income vanish, but it's the cost of living in a free and prosperous society. The dollars that disappear are highly visible to us, but we tend to take for granted the benefits we derive from their use.

In this chapter, we're not going to address the merits of all complaints about the convoluted American tax system – entire books have been written on the subject. However, we will take a brief exploratory trip through a few key topics: how our tax system works, how to minimize your taxes as much as possible, and how some tax-advantaged investment vehicles can be used to minimize your bill and put more money into your pockets. But first, let's get a little perspective.

Perspective Matters

We live in a free country where so many wonderful things are provided for us: our public schools educate our children, prompt healthcare is still easily accessible, infrastructure is far better than most places in the world, and emergency services like the fire department and police are ubiquitous and helpful. This is not to say that any of these systems are perfect – there are always things that can be fixed or improved upon. But compared to much of the rest of the world, America is incredibly rich and prosperous. And the benefits of these services – and the costs of paying for them – are still better than the alternative. As Oliver Wendell Holmes once said, "Taxes are the price we pay for living in a civilized society."

Many of the cultural boons we enjoy are funded by – you guessed it – taxes. So next time you are tempted to complain about tax rates or the messy process leading up to April 15, just remember to pause for a minute and count your blessings.

I'm not saying that the American tax system is ideal. There are many, many shortfalls, and I believe that the process is far more complicated that it needs to be. I dislike paying taxes just as much as the next guy. Combine the intricacies of the tax system with the bloated and bureaucratic ways of the Federal Government, and our system is far from perfect. But it's the only system we've got, so we might as well learn to work within its confines and use it to our advantage.

Disclaimer: I am in no way proposing that by "using the tax system to your advantage" you should lie, cheat, steal, or otherwise be dishonest about the taxes you owe. All I'm proposing is that we further our education about the tax system, understand how taxes work, and learn how to avoid overpaying our fair share. I've had to learn the hard way, and my ignorance has likely led me to overpaying on my taxes in years past. I paid my "dumb tax," so I want to help you avoid the same mistakes I've made. Knowledge is power – so I'm proposing that we grow in our knowledge about this important subject.

Understanding Tax Brackets

Perhaps the most fundamental item to understand is the concept of tax brackets. How much you pay in taxes depends on how much you make per year – which bracket you fall into. America's tax system has changed dramatically in recent years with the passage of President Trump's tax overhaul, but many of the fundamentals of the system remain the same.

America has a system that is known as a *progressive tax*, which means that the more you earn, the more you'll pay. Some countries have a flat tax, where everybody pays a flat percentage of their income, regardless of how much they earn. Others have regressive tax plans in which higher earners actually pay less of their income toward a tax bill (America's tax system has loopholes that allow for higher earners to pay less than some lower income earners, thanks to the types of income they earn from different sources, but we'll get into that later).

Here's a chart of the tax brackets for 2018:

Table 1. Tax Brackets and Rates, 2018

Rate	For Unmarried Individuals, Taxable Income Over	For Married Individuals Filing Joint Returns, Taxable Income Over	For Heads of Households, Taxable Income Over
10%	$0	$0	$0
12%	$9,525	$19,050	$13,600
22%	$38,700	$77,400	$51,800
24%	$82,500	$165,000	$82,500
32%	$157,500	$315,000	$157,500
35%	$200,000	$400,000	$200,000
37%	$500,000	$600,000	$500,000

As you can see from the chart, the more money you make in a given year, the higher of a percentage you'll pay. Those making under $9,524 per year pay 0% of their income in taxes, while those earning over $500,000 in a year pay the highest tax rate of all: 37%.

It's also important to note that the U.S. has what's known as a *marginal tax rate*, which means that once you cross the threshold from one rate to another, it's only the dollar amounts over the threshold that are taxed at a higher rate. For instance, after you make more than $38,700 you will jump from the 22% tax bracket to the 24% bracket, but only the amounts over $38,700 are taxed at 24%.

Aside from changing jobs, getting a significant raise, or establishing a side business for some extra income, people typically don't jump from one tax bracket to another (unless you're on the cusp of one). Finding out which tax bracket you're in is the first step to understanding taxes, but it certainly isn't the last: even after President Trump's recent tax overhaul, the American tax system is so confusing that it almost takes a Ph.D. to understand it. However, there are some common tactics you can use to minimize your tax bill and keep more of your money in your pocket, not the government's.

Who Is This IRA Guy, Anyway?

When it comes to taxes, you may hear the term IRA thrown around a lot – and rightly so. As we saw in our last chapter, establishing an investment strategy is incredibly important to building long-term wealth, but you always have to think about the tax implications of your investments. Fortunately, there are different types of accounts that can help you minimize your tax burden now or farther down the road.

IRA stands for *Individual Retirement Account*, and there are some significant tax benefits to opening one. Each dollar you contribute to an IRA (up to $5,500 per year) reduces your taxable income for the year, which means that you'll have a lower tax bill come April. For example, if you made $40,000 in 2018 and didn't contribute anything to an IRA, you'd be in the 22% tax bracket, making your tax bill $8,800 on April 15 (this does not take deductions and other special tax situations into account – we're just going after easy math).

However, if you made $40,000 a year and put $5,500 of that in an IRA, the Federal Government views your ordinary income as only *$34,500* for the year. There are two main benefits of contributing to an IRA with your income: you'll now get placed into a lower tax bracket (12% instead of 22%). This not only lowers your tax burden ($4,140 instead of $8,800), but you will have saved money for retirement in the process.

Even if you didn't get pushed into a lower tax bracket, using an IRA to reduce your taxable income is still a great strategy. Let's say you make $50,000 a year, which puts you into the 22% tax bracket. Contributing $5,500 to an IRA won't push you into a lower tax bracket this year, but that doesn't mean you won't reap any benefit: 22% of $44,500 is still less than 22% of $50,000, after all ($1,210 to be exact).

Traditional IRAs are considered *tax-deferred* accounts because your contributions lower your yearly taxable income, but they come with some rules. For instance, IRAs have penalties for early withdrawals (usually around 10%) although there are some exceptions, like withdrawing funds to make your first home purchase or fund education expenses. These penalties more or less force you into a long-term mindset, as it becomes significantly more expensive to make early withdrawals.

Also, don't think that you won't ever have to pay taxes on the funds inside a traditional IRA. That's why they're called tax-deferred accounts. You will still have to pay taxes when you with-draw money in retirement; however, an IRA can reduce your tax bill for each year that you pay into them, so often times it will end up being a wash. Depending on your financial situation, IRAs can be a great way to minimize your tax burden now and kick the proverbial "tax can" down the road. Always consult a tax professional when setting up an IRA or considering an early withdrawal.

Roth IRAs

Roth IRAs are another great way to save on taxes. The key differ-ence between a Roth IRA and a Traditional IRA is that Roth IRAs are funded using *after-tax* dollars, meaning they don't lower your taxable income for any contributions you make in a calendar year. However, they are not taxed *at all* when you with-draw your money at retirement. Roth IRA contributions, like their traditional IRA counterparts, are limited to $5,500 per year. If you make $40,000 a year and contribute $5,500 to your Roth IRA, your tax bill will still be calculated from your $40,000 of income. However, when that initial $5,500 has grown to several hundred thousand dollars when you retire, your tax bill will be zero. That's right: you won't owe any taxes and can withdraw all of your hard-earned money completely tax-free. Taking advantage of compounding while minimizing taxes farther down the road feels good.

There are some other key differences, too: Roth IRAs don't require you to take disbursements at retirement age like traditional IRAs do, and unlike many 401(k)s offered by employers, Roth IRAs are self-managed. You can't count on the HR department at your workplace to manage the IRA for you – you must do the work of selecting investments, rebalancing, and adjusting your stock/bond allocation over time. But if you stay educated, invest wisely, and rebalance yearly, you'll have a big nest egg waiting for you when you retire – again, 100% tax-free.

Popular "Robo-Advisors" like Betterment have expanded in recent years to offer IRAs (both Traditional and Roth) as part of their services, so it may be worth opening up a retirement account with a service like Betterment to take advantage of their tax loss harvesting, tax-coordinated portfolios, and more.

Deductions and Credits

If you're self-employed, own your own business, or have the proverbial "side hustle," deductions are a great way to minimize your tax bill. The government knows that certain expenses are necessary for running a business: office space, tangible assets, business travel, software, and more. If you engage in these activities or spend any money on items necessary to run your business, the government will let you deduct those from your ordinary income, effectively lowering your taxable income, and in turn, your tax bill. It's important to be honest and keep receipts and documentation of all your spending. You can't just make up business expenses by pulling them out of thin air when it's convenient. Using software like QuickBooks Self-Employed can help you out in this arena.

Many young people don't keep track of deductions, which could be detrimental to their tax bill come April. Especially with the recent Trump tax reform and its changes to deductions, it's more profitable for many people to take the standard deduction rather than itemizing their deductions, but your tax situation may vary. I prefer to itemize my deductions every year – even if the standard deduction saves me more money, I still like having a grasp on how much I'm spending to operate my business.

And if you aren't self-employed, don't worry. There are a number of personal deductions and credits that you can take to lower your tax bill, including tax preparation fees, losses due to theft or casualty, education credits, costs associated with moving for a job, and more. Many people choose the "Standard Deduction" rather than itemizing these deductions, but it always pays to keep track of your expenses to have the best chance at lowering your tax bill as you can.

Charitable Giving

Have you ever given money to a non-profit organization, dropped off some unwanted household items at Goodwill, or tithed to your church? Provided that you're donating to a recognized 501(c)(3) non-profit organization, all of these actions are tax-deductible and can save you money on your taxes.

This one isn't too complicated, and most people know about it. The thing most people don't know is that contributions are limited to 50% of your annual income, and that any additional giving above this amount carries forward to the next year.

If you made $100,000 a year, your tax bill would be $24,000 (24% of $100,000). But, if you were able to give away half of your income, your tax bill would only be $11,000 (22% of $50,000), and anything donated above and beyond 50% of your income would carry forward to the next year, so you could reap tax benefits in the future as well.

Very few people can afford to give away half of their income and still make ends meet for the year, but if you have a significant financial event (like selling a company, cashing out on some equity, etc), this can be a great strategy to help others while minimizing your tax bill in the current year and for years to come. The important thing with donations is to always get a receipt of your donation – this will be necessary if (God forbid) you're ever audited.

But Wait, There's More!

There are scores of tax breaks available, from contributing to Health Savings Accounts to buying an electric vehicle, to counting the costs of hunting for a new job, or even for having a child (hopefully you're not just having a kid for the tax benefit). Tax laws and deductions are always changing, so we're not going to spend time delving into the other common tax breaks here.

Just be sure to do some research online, or contact a local tax professional or CPA if you need help on your taxes or have questions about which breaks you can qualify for in order to lower your tax bill. There are opportunities for tax savings for nearly everyone, and your money is better-off in your pockets than in Uncle Sam's.

Estimated Quarterly Taxes

The so-called "Gig Economy" is on the rise, especially among Millennials and younger workers. According to the U.S. Government Accountability Office, 40.4% of the American workforce is now made up of "contingent workers" – that is, people who may not have what we traditionally consider secure jobs. Not all of these workers are entirely self-employed, but due to their employment arrangements many of these Americans will not fall into a traditional tax situation; therefore, they may have to deal with a nuance of the American tax system: estimated taxes. If you derive a significant portion or all of your income from being self-employed (as I do), the government treats you a little differently.

For most people, taxes are fairly easy and don't take much time to complete. Many people will have a W-2 from their employer, which states how much money they made and how much money their employer withheld from their paychecks to pay for taxes. Everyone who is self-employed will receive 1099 forms from a variety of different "employers." These forms are different, because we are not *employees* of these organizations, but rather *independent contractors* who were hired to perform a specific job or service. As a result, our taxes are not withheld from our paychecks by our "employers," which means we'll need to set some money aside to pay our tax bill.

The government is just like you and me: it likes its money, and it wants it now. As a result, independent contractors and others who are self-employed don't just pay their taxes on April 15: we have to pay quarterly taxes. If you're self-employed, you'll need to pay the Federal Government a quarter of your overall estimated tax bill every three months. This amount is calculated from previous tax returns.

Many self-employed freelancers and other creative professionals can see their incomes fluctuate quite a bit, so their quarterly tax payments may be high or low depending on changes in income. Even if your income increases dramatically next year, your quarterly payments are viewed as *safe harbor* payments – as long as you're paying the amount the government says you will actually owe, the government won't penalize you if your quarterly tax payments amount to less than what you owe in a given year (but you will have to make up the difference in April). I found this one out the hard way and almost missed making my estimated tax payments. Thank goodness I asked a CPA, who clarified that I had to pay taxes every quarter, or else I could have been in a heap of trouble.

Quarterly taxes used to be stressful for me: the months of January, April, June, and September (when quarterly payments are due) were a little leaner than other months, and more than a little stressful. However, I now have a system in place that helps me adequately deal with these tax payments. At the end of every week, I use a spreadsheet to track how much I've received that week in the form of checks and online payments. I primarily use this spreadsheet to track how much money I am setting aside for savings and tithing to my church, but in one column, I have predefined amounts to track quarterly taxes. I could do this every month, but I've found that a shorter feedback loop helps me have a better gauge on how my business is performing and helps me establish this good habit. For instance, I know that there are eight weeks between April 15 and June 15 (when my next quarterly payment is due), so I transfer a set amount of money each week until the next due date into a separate tax account, always keeping track of the totals in my spreadsheet. This functions like withholding on a paycheck – rather than being stressed about quarterly payments every three months, I set some money aside weekly to make these payments to eliminate stress and make sure the money is there. If you are self-employed or have to face estimated taxes, I'd recommend doing the same.

Keep It All In Perspective

Aside from CPAs and IRS agents, very few people get excited about taxes. Nobody likes to see a smaller paycheck every two weeks, or to make a large payment every quarter. Tax refunds that some people get in April are nice, but I'm guessing that most people would like to lessen the amount of taxes they pay (if not doing away with them entirely). Looked at another way, any refund you receive from the government was actually an interest-free loan from you to them.

And yet, taxes are a fact of life. Whenever I'm tempted to complain about taxes, my wife always reminds me to put it all in perspective: as we've mentioned previously, our country is free and prosperous in so many ways, and many of the everyday essentials we take for granted are funded by taxes. Not all of these systems are perfect, but their benefits far outweigh the downside or the lack of vital services that don't exist in countries without a stable tax base. So when considering taxes, it's important to have a bit of perspective, and when paying them, it's helpful to know how to use the system to your advantage.

It's my hope that this primer on taxes will help you plan

better, minimize your tax bill, and reap the rewards along your financial journey.

Before You Move On

Before you move on, take a minute to assess your tax situation for the upcoming year. If you're a salaried employee who receives a W-2, this probably won't take long. But if you have any self-employment income or have to pay estimated taxes this year, take a minute to come up with a strategy for paying them. Doing so will help you be more prepared for the upcoming tax year, and hopefully experience less stress about the topic.

———

PREPARATION for all of life's expenses, not just taxes, is incredibly important. Unfortunately, it's a skill so many of us lack, especially when we are young, which is why we will now turn our attention to one of the most important practices to develop as a Millennial: the skill of budgeting.

Chapter 6

BUDGETING MATTERS

OK, BUDGETING SUCKS. HERE'S HOW TO MAKE
IT SUCK LESS.

A hh, the budget: the bane of many American households' existence, and certainly one of the most loathed words for a twenty-something or recent college grad. For most people, budgeting sucks. Perhaps for you, "budget" seems like a dirty word. Perhaps you grew up in a family where life was ruled by the Almighty Budget and in time you came to resent it. Maybe it's the opposite – maybe the money flowed so freely that the concept of sticking to a budget seems foreign and undesirable.

There's no way around it: budgeting is neither sexy nor fun. For many, it's just a symbol of financial repression – the only purpose a budget seems to serve is to keep us longing for the days when we can advance in our jobs, reach our financial goals, and relish our financial freedom by sitting on the beach sipping a Mai Tai.

But budgets don't have to be a symbol of repression or evoke disdain. In fact, budgets are perhaps the best way for us to realize our financial goals. Done correctly, budgeting can actually bring freedom.

Budgets = Freedom

The problem with most people who hate budgets (especially people in their twenties) is that they equate having a budget with being cheap. In their minds, if you have a budget, you're slave to a strict set of rules, an arbitrary document that dictates how and when you spend your money. Most people think of a budget as prison bars holding them back from a "rich and satisfying" life of spending their money however they please. It's like having a parent stand over your shoulder 24/7, scolding you for less-than-optimal financial choices.

The phenomenon of wild, unrestrained spending that so many young people are prone to often gets worse when they go off to college. Emancipated from parental restrictions and over-sight, there's unparalleled freedom to go wild. A number of questionable choices can be and often are made during college, and many of them carry dire financial consequences. For those who never learned how to properly budget their money to make it last, living on their own is the ultimate temptation to spend money on anything and everything. Their newfound freedom is sweet…until the bill arrives.

I should know. My first year of college, I watched a healthy $1500 balance dwindle down to less than $100 in a matter of months. What did I spend my money on? For the life of me, I couldn't tell you. What I do know is that I lacked financial self-control in the worst way possible. College was ripe with opportunities for fun and adventure – and I took advantage of them –

but without a job or self-control when it came to my spending habits, I was living an (admittedly fun) lifestyle that was unsustainable.

That's what I wish I knew as a freshman in college: a budget means freedom. It didn't need to look like a complex spreadsheet with every metric imaginable – there wasn't that much I could actually spend my money on, after all – but a rough set of guidelines on how much I could safely spend in a month would have gone a long way in helping me hold on to my hard-earned money while still making time for the fun opportunities that college years bring.

What's Important to You?

A budget isn't meant to be a strict set of rules that takes away your freedom. Instead, it's meant to be a pre-defined plan that prioritizes what's most important to you, and therefore, what you choose to spend your money on.

There are some things we can't live without. We all need a place to live, groceries, transportation, and the occasional night out. Each of these items should always find a place in our budget. But when we get down to it, the question of *what's really important to you?* is the most, well, *important* question you can ask when setting up a budget. After you account for the necessities, asking yourself what's most important – which variable you want to optimize for – will cause your budget to naturally evolve and will help you prioritize whichever goals are most important to you.

I have friends who love their homes. Their home is their sanctuary, the place they return to every day to unwind. For them, spending money on furnishings and home improvement is a no-brainer, while to others, it's an unnecessary luxury. I know of others who absolutely love food and wine, but they don't care as much where they live. For them, a minimal amount spent on housing every month isn't a problem or even a burden, because it frees them up to spend money on other things like experiencing the very best dining experiences imaginable.

25-year old Brandon understands this well. He's an engineer at Google, where he makes well over $100,000 per year. That may seem like a lot of money, but housing in the San Francisco Bay Area is unbelievably expensive. Brandon didn't want to waste his salary on an expensive apartment, so he got a little creative with his budget and how he used the money he was making. So what did Brandon do? Upon joining Google as a software engineer, he spent his $10,000 signing bonus on a 16-foot box truck. It's more than just a mode of transportation: for Brandon, the truck is his home. Literally.

Rather than spending $2,500 or more per month on a basic one-bedroom apartment close to work, Brandon sleeps every night in Google's parking lot. "I realized I was paying an exorbitant amount of money for the apartment I was staying in — and I was almost never home," he says. "It's really hard to justify throwing that kind of money away. You're essentially burning it – you're not putting equity in anything and you're not building it up for a future. That was really hard for me to reconcile."

Brandon understands the concept that creative budgeting means more freedom for what is important to him. According to him, "I don't need an apartment – I just need a bed and a place to put it. I'd heard about other people trying similarly silly things, so I did a bit of research and figured I'd give it a shot."

Other than a $121/month insurance bill for the truck, Brandon's expenses are close to zero. The truck was paid for in cash, he doesn't use electricity, and he's able to eat all of his meals and even shower on Google's campus. As a result, he's been able to save over 90% of his salary for long-term financial goals. He still goes out with friends, using Uber or public transportation to get him where he needs to go. Thanks to a permanent spot in Google's parking lot, he saves hours' worth of commuting time every day. Oh, and that $22,434 of student debt he was responsible for upon graduation? He paid it off in under a year.

Granted, this is not a strategy that's available (or even advisable) for everyone. Balance is important. Our living and relational circumstances will often dictate just how much fun we can have with our budget and the ways in which we spend our money. But for a 25-year old single guy to earn over $100,000 – and keep more than 90% of it – it's certainly a creative move.

See what I mean? Creative thinking when you are budgeting doesn't have to mean restricting what you can spend your money on. It means freedom, and you can get really imaginative.

Make Room for Fun

A great way to form a new budgeting habit is to put a little bit of fun in it – determine what's important to you, and make it fun. Spending money from time to time on things that make you happy can motivate you to keep your spending habits in check in other areas. As co-author of *The Financial Diaries* Rachel Schneider says, "Allowing yourself a pocket where you lack discipline apparently makes it easier to be disciplined everywhere else."

It's important to explicitly build fun into your budget, though – don't just wing it. You need to have a specific number built into your budget. If not, you may have to rely on your own willpower, which is dangerous.

In 1998, psychologist Roy Baumeister of Case Western University set out to test people's willpower. In the study, Baumeister kept participants in a room that smelled like freshly baked chocolate cookies and then teased them further by showing them a plate of cookies and other chocolate-flavored confections. Some participants did get to indulge, while others (whose resolve was being tested) were asked to eat radishes instead. Unsurprisingly, many of the radish-eaters "exhibited clear interest in the chocolates, to the point of looking longingly at the chocolate display and in a few cases even picking up the cookies to sniff at them."

The team then gave the participants a second, supposedly unrelated exercise – they asked them to complete a puzzle. The results? Those who ate radishes spent less than half the time trying to solve the puzzle compared to their chocolate-eating companions.

In other words, those who had to rely on their willpower to resist the cookies could no longer find the energy to fully engage in another torturous task. Apparently, our willpower is like a muscle: it can be depleted, so we must set up systems and structures that reduce our reliance on willpower alone whenever possible.

So, make room for fun in your budget, but don't just wing it or rely on your willpower – have a plan.

The Coffee Guy

My obsession with coffee began in college – not out of necessity like so many of my peers, but rather out of habit. I had never enjoyed coffee before arriving at college, but the convenience of a Keurig in my dorm room soon made coffee an everyday ritual for me.

Eventually, I became "enlightened" to the wonderful coffee that was available through the various craft coffee shops around town, so I began going out to coffee on a regular basis. The Keurig was eventually replaced by a trip to my favorite coffee shop, The French Press, every morning where I'd usually get a mocha or a pour-over (two of the more expensive items on the menu).

These costs added up over time. While coffee, gasoline, and the occasional meal out were my only real expenses at that point in college, and because I was working part-time for a non-profit, I was able to save money during this process. Among my friends, I quickly gained a reputation for my morning coffee habit. I was officially "the coffee guy."

Some of my peers may have thought that I was spending too much money on coffee, and looking back, they were probably right. I could have gotten coffee for much cheaper by buying beans and making coffee in my room, or by drinking coffee at the Dining Commons, but for my newfound love of great coffee, neither of these options would do. Coffee was important to me – it was a nice way to enjoy some time to myself in the early morning before the craziness of college life took hold of the day. I had chosen to prioritize a trip to get coffee every morning, and I had budgeted it in, so it was fine. That meant more of my budget for the month went to coffee shops, but I don't regret it at all. It suited my lifestyle and was important to me, so I made sure to prioritize it in my budget.

Fast-forward several years and I don't go out to coffee nearly as much – certainly not every morning. I get coffee with one of my roommates from college every Tuesday morning, and occasionally my wife and I will go on a coffee date, but other than that I make most of my coffee at home. Now because my life situation has changed (we have more expenses now, and I've learned to be just as satisfied by brewing a cup of coffee at home), my wife and I spend about $50 per month on coffee – far from the $150 or more I used to spend.

Budgets and Backpacking

Some college friends of mine chose to hike the Pacific Coast Trail a few years back. Stretching over 2,700 miles from Mexico to Canada, this world-renowned trail is a magnet for outdoor adventure-lovers and backpacking fanatics who attempt to hike it from end-to-end each year.

My friends' trip lasted over 6 months – they left in May and didn't finish until October. Their typical day consisted of 15-20 miles of hiking, stopping in nearby towns for pizza and beer (or anything that wasn't freeze-dried, I imagine) when they were able. They re-supplied by having friends and family members sign up to send packages at strategic points in their journey. To many, this would seem crazy.

But really, it's not that crazy. Thousands of people make similar treks each year. To be one of the few who have hiked from Mexico to Canada is a badge of honor, a rare feat that only the most dedicated outdoorsmen and women have accomplished. What *would* be crazy is going into a journey like that blind: without a hiking plan, a re-supply plan, or ways to contact friends and family, their exciting journey could have quickly spiraled into disaster.

But these guys had a plan. They knew how much they were going to hike, when they were going to stop, and when they could expect supplies and care-packages along the way. They spent time beforehand carefully planning and strategizing their trip…much like having a budget.

Their plan allowed for flexibility in their schedules – they were able to hike extra if they had the energy, stop in a town for a few days along the way and enjoy a real bed every once in a while, or "splurge" on things that are real luxuries when appropriate (I'm guessing they have an appreciation for pizza and beer that surpasses that of most people).

The lesson we can learn from them is to think about a budget not as a constricting, rigid creation that limits our freedom but rather as a plan – a roadmap that will help us get to where we want to go faster and more effectively. If my two friends wouldn't dare embark on their 2,700-mile journey without a basic plan, why would any of us set off on the winding, uncertain path of our financial lives without a basic framework to guide us?

Budgeting: The Numbers

When we look at the numbers, it's not so surprising that few people understand how to budget well, primarily because so few people bother to budget at all. According to a 2013 Gallup poll, only 32% of U.S. households prepare a monthly budget. Why do we not prepare for our financial well-being if deep down we understand its importance?

A healthy budgeting habit may have something to do with level of education. While 38% of college-educated households have a budgeting habit, only 26% of those with a high school degree have a budget, yet data shows that they will earn less over their lifetimes, and so planning will be more important. The lack of budgeting may be explained by a number of factors, including a desire to avoid thinking about uncomfortable choices found in budgets, or incomes that are high enough to allow for discretionary spending without having to track every dollar.

But for those of us who do budget, where do we spend our money? In a typical household, the largest expense for many is housing, accounting for 33% of total household spending. Transportation (17%), food (12.5%), and insurance costs (11.3%) take the next largest pieces of the pie.

Healthcare is another major factor. As costs increase, healthcare spending is on the rise: medical spending rose more than 34% over the past decade. Healthcare spending accounts for a larger share of our budgets than it did in the past, although the total yearly cost is still under 10% of income. We can see from these numbers that we spend a lot of money on the essentials – and yet, there is still a lot of room in our budgets for what is most important to us.

It's also worth noting how budgets have changed over time. For example, housing has become much more expensive: according to the U.S. Bureau of Labor Statistics, in the early 1900s the average family spent 42.5% of their budgets on food and only 23% on housing. Today, housing accounts for 33% of our spending, and food has decreased in cost as a percentage of our budgets by a factor of four. One hundred years ago, more than 67% of spending was on these two categories, while today they comprise less than 50% of our budgets.

As we saw from Chapter 3, an important line item in our budgets is *savings* – but how well do most of us do at saving for a rainy day? The average American has less than $1,000 set aside in savings, a phenomenon that is fueled by our low savings rates. As of 2014, Americans only saved 4.3% of their income on average. This is far below the long-term average of 10% that existed in the 1950s, and far beneath what most families need to be saving to fend off unplanned expenses and enjoy an on-time retirement. What's worse: nearly 1 in 3 Americans (29.2%) aren't saving any of their income at all.

Here's an infographic showing the average budget categories for the typical American family:

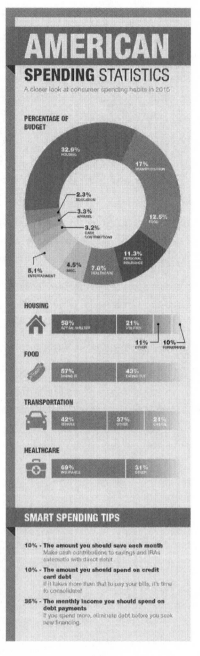

How Well Do We Actually Stick to Our Budgets?

Now that we've seen the numbers, the question then becomes: how well do people stick to their budgets? A Bankrate study performed in 2015 concludes that while a good number of households have a budget, sticking to it is not a habit we tend to nurture. Instead, we rely on *mental accounting*, a tactic that can lead us astray. "Mental accounting is really unreliable and prone to mathematical mistakes and rationalizations," says Claes Bell of Bankrate. Combined with lackluster saving habits and a lack of financial certainty, "for many, a financial downward spiral is just one emergency-room visit away," says Bell.

New technologies can actually have negative effects on our propensity to stick to our budgets. Research has shown that the ubiquity of credit cards and other cashless technologies like ApplePay and Android Pay actually cause us to spend more than we would have with another payment method, such as cash. Combine this with the fact that we rarely ever check our budgets to see how much money is available for groceries, entertainment, or other discretionary expenses, and it's not a surprise that so many Americans struggle to stay on budget.

Millennials and Money: How Much Do We Have, and How Much Room is There?

So what does this mean for Millennials and young twenty-some-things? How do we spend our money, and how can we improve our budgeting habits to have more left over?

A *Time* study of recent college graduates between the ages of 25 and 34 reveals how younger generations tend to spend their money. The households in this study typically had two adults and one child under the age of 18. Average total household income was $54,622 after taxes for this group, about $4,552 per month. By and large, the budgets and spending habits of this age group do not look much different than those in older generations, with the exception of how much money they have left over. After covering all essentials (housing, food, transportation, and health-care) and after accounting for typical entertainment and discretionary expenses, the average young household is left over with $423 per month. Depending on your perspective and your financial situation, that number may sound like a little or a lot, but that equates to saving $5,076 per year, a savings rate of 9.3%.

These numbers sound positive at first – *more than double the national savings rate!* – but when we look further, we can see the financial implications. If we assume this hypothetical couple is 30 years old and is able to save $5,076 per year until they retire at age 67, assuming a market return of 9% per year, this hypothetical couple will have $484,000 at retirement.

These assumptions are clearly optimistic: typical retirements happen earlier than 67, and as we've seen, the stock market has an historical long-term return of 6.6%. Given these known quantities, it's highly likely that this couple will have significantly less than $484,000 available to them at retirement.

And yet, the typical couple will require far more: according to a 2017 Merrill Lynch study, the average cost of retirement in America has risen to $738,400. Keep in mind, these are only averages – retirees accustomed to higher incomes and higher standards of living may need even more to maintain their lifestyles in retirement, while others will require less. So, unfortunately, unless this couple adjusts their savings substantially, they may find themselves coming up *more than a quarter of a million dollars short.*

It's factual information like this that highlight the importance of budgeting, especially when you're so young. Without an ability to analyze concrete data, you're essentially playing a high-stakes guessing game – and your wager is your future.

How to Make A Good Budget

So if you want to have enough money to make ends meet every month and you'd like to comfortably retire at a reasonable age, what's the best way to do it?

There are many ways to craft a budget, and none are more "right" than the others, but I'd like to propose an experiment that may help you see the differences in your perception of how much you're spending and how much you're *actually* spending. To begin, start by using estimates to determine what you think you're spending in each main category. Some of these will be easy to quantify: you probably know off the top of your head what your rent payments are, about how much you spend on groceries every month, etc. But other categories may elude you: just how much *are* you spending on entertainment? Is your budget for eating out way out of whack? Does travel eat up way more of your budget than you think is reasonable? Don't consult past financial statements or receipts for this step – just make a guess.

Once you have outlined your guesses, go back to your bank and credit card statements and find out what your spending actually is for a typical month. Compare these real numbers to the guesses you just made. Are there any huge discrepancies? Doing so may allow you to discover new ways to save money where you hadn't thought possible before.

Maybe you're spending way too much money on eating out when those dollars should be allocated towards groceries. Maybe you were expecting your transportation expenses to be much higher and there's wiggle room in the budget. Feel free to repurpose those dollars to a category that's more important to you, like setting money aside for investments or splurging on something you've been wanting to buy for a while. As long as you don't forget about important items such as saving for retirement and contributing to your emergency fund (yes, these need to be line items in your budget every month), you'll be good to go. As Warren Buffett once said, "Do not save what is left after spending – spend what is left after saving."

Addressing our perceptions and how they may deviate from reality is a good exercise to discover more about our attitudes toward money – and the results may be surprising. However, crafting a budget is accomplished in a few easy steps (and yes, these are *in order* – don't skip over one step just to get to another that seems more fun!):

1. **Income.** Add up all sources of income, from paychecks to odd jobs to selling things online – this is the absolute maximum number of dollars you can spend in a given month.
2. **Essentials.** Add up your fixed expenses, like rent payments, car payments, groceries, etc. These are essential expenses you can't live without.
3. **Debt.** Next, account for any debt repayments you have. This could include student loans, car loans (if you already counted this in the "essentials" category, that's fine), or credit card payments.

4. **Savings.** Don't forget to account for things like Emergency Fund contributions, or if you're able, contributions to retirement. If you don't account for savings in your budget, you'll never save any. The money won't save itself!

5. **Fun.** If you still have money left over after providing for your essential needs, repaying debt, and contributing to savings, go wild! This is where you can determine what is most important to you and choose to spend this money accordingly. Want to eat out a lot? Go for it. Want to use this money to travel? Why not? Some people choose to put this extra "fun money" right back into savings, while others want to spend more on fun experiences. What you choose to do with your hard-earned money is up to you. You've worked for it – now go enjoy it!

Using the Data

The most important part of budgeting is to actually use the data you are given. You can't make good or accurate decisions without data, because you have no empirical evidence on which to back up your hypotheses. If you don't have tangible data to fall back on, your assumptions about how you're spending your money could be dead wrong.

This happened to me a few months ago. I was appalled at how much money my wife and I were spending on groceries. It was more than I had ever spent on groceries before, and I was convinced that we needed to make a change in order to save money...until I looked at our budget, that is. Not only were our grocery bills consistent with what we had been spending in the past, but they didn't account for a large percentage of our monthly spending at all – groceries were a relatively small part of our budget, whereas there were ample opportunities to cut unnecessary expenditures elsewhere. My brain was playing tricks on me, and my "mental accounting" was all wrong. By consulting the data, I was able to get a more accurate picture of our spending and where our money was actually going.

Incidentally, the same thing happened with our utilities bill. It was fairly cold this winter, and we had been running our heater more than we usually do. As a result, our natural gas bill increased *over 500%* from one month to another! The overall bill was still fairly inexpensive, but it was the principle of such a huge increase that had me up in arms. In protest, I turned our heater off in order to save money (in my defense, it was starting to get warm again). My wife thought I was being ridiculous (she's usually right). When we consulted our budget and graphed our spending as a pie chart, our utilities were so small that they didn't even register as a part of the graph. The data had spoken, and I was wrong. I swallowed my pride and turned the heater back on.

How to Stick to Your Budget

Creating a budget is relatively straightforward. Sticking to your budget is another matter. There are countless apps and services out there that seek to help you stick to your established budget, but in the end, it all comes down to self-discipline and creating habits that reinforce positive behavior.

To adhere to discipline and create new habits, perhaps it's most helpful to begin with the end in mind. Think about what would happen if you didn't stick to your budget. Try it: just picture yourself a year from now, but imagine that you didn't stick to your budget. As a result, you are even more in debt and the interest payments are adding up quickly, you weren't able to use time to your advantage in making investments and planning for the future, and you are even more stressed than usual about money. Doesn't feel good, does it?

Now, take a step back and visualize the process of actively sticking to your budget. Imagine what steps you will take when you go to buy something online or in person. The first question you should ask yourself is this: *do I really need this?* If the answer is truly yes, you will then check your budget on an app like Mint, or a spreadsheet you have on your phone. If money is available, you can make the purchase. If not, it's decision time: you can either move some money around from line items that have a surplus, or you can implement a plan to make your purchase after you have the money, perhaps a few weeks or a few months in the future.

Another great way to create a habit of sticking to your budget is to set a goal for yourself which will force you to begin with the end in mind. Choose a goal that only budgeting can help you obtain, whether it be fully funding your emergency fund, saving for a big purchase or a special vacation, or eliminating credit card debt entirely. Such goals help create motivation because the motivation for sticking to your budget isn't because of what some guy in a book told you to do – you're sticking to your budget for a specific reason. Think about how good it will feel to accomplish your goal…and then remind yourself of that feeling and sense of accomplishment every time you pull out your credit card to make a purchase. Research has shown that establishing goals for yourself (for instance, paying off all of your credit card debt within 12 months) is the very best way to actually achieve them and reinforce brand new habits. What better place to start than budgeting?

Why You Should Stick to Your Budget

Although budgets can seem limiting, there are many reasons to utilize a budget and stick to it. First and foremost, budgets are the best way to achieve your financial goals, regardless of what goals they may be. Without a budget it's incredibly difficult, if not impossible, to obtain unbiased, concrete figures about your income, spending habits, and where your money is going. If you want more control over your money, a good budget is the first place you should start.

Secondly, budgets enable a level of financial achievement that is not available to people without them. Yes, "financial achievement" is somewhat tied to income; however, for those whose income grows over time but financial independence seems always out-of-reach, a budget is the best solution. One of the most compelling arguments for budgeting comes from a study of more than 7,000 U.S. adults by the Center for Financial Services Innovation (CFSI). Holding all other factors constant, the CFSI found that households with a planned savings habit tied to budgeting were *four times more likely* to be financially healthy than other families (that is, able to pay their bills on time, stay out of debt, invest for the long-term, have adequate insurance, etc). What's more, people who planned ahead to make sure they had enough money to pay large, irregular expenses were *ten times more likely* to be in good shape financially. If you don't have the numbers on your side, you can't make a good plan – and the lack of a good plan usually has serious consequences.

Ever heard of the term "lifestyle inflation"? It's the reason why so many high earners aren't getting ahead. Recent figures indicate that 1 in 10 Americans earning more than $100,000 per year are living paycheck to paycheck and are struggling to make ends meet. To the extent that this phenomenon is due to student debt repayments (many earning over $100,000 have an advanced degree in their field and lots of school debt to pay off), this may be understandable. But if an inability to make ends meet at such a high income is due to lifestyle inflation, this number is shocking.

There's a belief that budgeting is only a problem for the lower and middle classes. The more money you make, the less money becomes a problem or stressor in your life, right? Not even close. According to a 2015 study by GOBankingRates, budgeting is the top money challenge for workers earning $100,000 to $149,000 annually, and the second-most pressing issue for those earning $150,000 or more. "People who are earning $100,000 or more you would think are not worried as much about money," said Cameron Huddleston of GOBankingRates. "The truth is, the more we earn, the more many people end up spending." Whether you're earning $20,000 a year or $200,000 a year, budgeting can still be a challenge. Adherence to a thoughtful budget is the best way to increase your chances of financial achievement and financial independence.

In our twenties, our financial goals may not yet be very well-developed, and financial independence likely isn't at the forefront of our minds. But if we adopt a long-term mindset, we'll see that learning the skill of budgeting at an early age is a crucial skill, since it helps us set up a better financial future. The better you become at budgeting, the more informed you are and the more options you will have at your disposal. It's those who do not develop a budgeting habit and who do not have the data they need to make wise decisions who are more likely to fall into debt or fail to save for the future.

The more used to budgeting we are, the better our chances of keeping debt low and realizing financial independence at an earlier age. Put simply, if we want to thrive – to retire early (or even on time for that matter), bless other people philanthropically, or provide for a standard of living later in life that is beyond our current capacity, the best way to do so is by cultivating a budgeting habit when we are young.

At their essence, budgets are all about simplicity and freedom. Having a budget doesn't mean you're cheap – it means you're thoughtful. If you learn the skills necessary to cultivate a budgeting habit at an early age, financial thoughtfulness will compound over time, just like interest, which will enable you to reap rewards far greater than your peers.

Before You Move On

Before you move on to the next chapter, make sure you've created a budget (for a list of financial tools I recommend, visit www.moneyformillennialsbook.com). Depending on how many expenses you have, this process may take a few hours. Be sure to use the basic framework for budgets we looked at in this chapter:

1. Start with **Income.**
2. Account for **Essentials.**
3. Prioritize **Debt Repayment.**
4. Don't Forget **Savings.**

5. **Spend** What's Left Over.

———

Now that you've established a budgeting habit, our exploration of how best to use money in your twenties turns to a topic that faces the vast majority of Millennials and far too many who are older than us: debt.

Chapter 7

HOW TO DEAL WITH DEBT

NOT ALL DEBT IS BAD. BUT MOST OF IT IS.

Debt: the scourge of modern America. The cause of financial crises the likes of which the world had never seen before. The downfall of so many American families who are struggling to keep their heads above water. The second-leading cause of divorce. A major contributor to depression and increased risk of suicide. According to *Forbes*, one in four Americans have PTSD-like symptoms from financial stress, much of which is caused by high levels of debt. From Fortune 500 corporations to recent college grads, we don't know how to manage our debt, and it's killing us.

As of 2017, the average American family has more than $133,568 of debt. Mortgage debt accounts for a large percentage of this, which is not necessarily a bad thing (the average American who owns a home has a $178,037 mortgage balance). A house is an investment, after all.

Student debt is on the rise, too. As of 2017, the average American college grad has more than $47,047 in debt, while graduate students on average take on an additional $40,229 for their studies. Student debt for Millennials is worse than it traditionally has been for older generations both in real terms and as a percentage of their income: Millennials have taken on an average of 300% more student debt than their parents. Just as with mortgages, this debt isn't necessarily bad debt – education is a investment – but there are some caveats. For instance, 56% of Millennials with student loans have delayed a major life event like getting married or having kids because of their debt.

However, personal debt like credit card debt accounts for a huge percentage of bad debts – the average American has more than $15,983 of credit card debt, and pays more than $904 of interest per year. This is money that could be used for other purposes like savings or investments, but is instead being used to service debt. Either as a result of poor financial planning, job loss, lack of emergency savings, or gross overconsumption that exceeds income, our society is absolutely drowning in debt. An overwhelming majority of Millennials – more than 62% – now hold more debt than money saved. As Andrew Allentuck of Canada's *Financial Post* notes, "The problem is cash myopia – insecurity and a desire for liquidity often go together." If we want to thrive as a society, or if we simply desire to achieve personal financial independence, getting out of debt should be our #1 priority.

What Debt Does to Our Brains

Chances are that you know someone who is in debt right now. Actually, chances are that you *are* that person in debt. According to a study of household indebtedness in the United States, more than 4 out of 10 American household are in some form of significant personal debt (this number excludes mortgages, which are backed by an asset).

Yet despite our debt, we're unlikely to reach out to friends and family as a support network. It's not just that we don't want to ask for money – even talking about our debt is a big no-no. Like it or not, talking about debt is a cultural taboo, so we hesitate to bring it up. As Brad Klontz, a financial psychologist who teaches at Creighton University says, "You are more likely to hear from your buddy that he is on Viagra than that he has credit-card problems. Much more likely."

But our collective silence about debt is imposing a huge burden on our health and well-being. People in significant debt report themselves as being less satisfied, less happy, and more stressed, overwhelmed, and burdened by the dollar signs hanging over their heads. They feel enslaved, trapped in a cycle of debt repayment and high interest rates that prevent them from getting ahead.

Dr. John Gathergood surveyed more than 3,000 households in the U.K. in an effort to find out the effects financial illiteracy have on one's future financial health. He found that misunderstanding debt and being financially illiterate led to the accrual of even more debt. In a separate survey of 10,000 people in the U.K., Gathergood found that people who struggle to pay off their loans are more than twice as likely to experience a host of mental health problems ranging from depression to severe anxiety. Similar studies back up Dr. Gathergood's findings. Lawrence M. Berger of the University of Wisconsin, in a paper entitled "Household Debt and Adult Depressive Symptoms" found that short-term personal debt – comprised mainly of credit card debt and overdue bills – is associated with "greater depression and stress, declining quality of marital relations and parenting behavior, and adverse child outcomes."

The burden of debt isn't just bad for our wallets or our financial future: it actually degrades our brains, our relationships, and our satisfaction with life. It's clear that if we want to live a healthy life (emotionally, spiritually, and financially), we should focus on eliminating debt to the best of our ability.

But how can we do so? First, we need to know the difference between the various types of debt.

Good Debt, Bad Debt, and Knowing the Difference

Not all debt is created equal: there are good debts and there are bad debts. But what's the difference between the two? Put simply, there are some things that are worth going into debt for. These include items that are absolutely necessary for daily life, like a home to live in or a car to drive to your place of employment (but only if you absolutely need a car and are unable to pay in cash). Higher education and student loans also fall into this category, as the jobs and incomes available to a college graduate usually significantly exceed those available to high school graduates. With a mortgage, you're investing in an asset that both provides a place for you and your family to live and one that can – and usually does – grow in value over time. By taking on student loans, you're investing in your education and obtaining skills that can help you obtain higher-paying jobs in fields where such a degree is necessary (since the future earning power far exceeds the debt incurred). Managed properly, good debt can be beneficial to your long-term job prospects, earning potential, and net worth.

Car loans can be a bit of a different story. They aren't necessarily "good" debt, but they may not be terrible, either. It is most likely necessary to have a car to take you to and from your job – your vehicle is something that allows you to have that source of income, so it's not 100% bad. But too many people mistake a car for an asset, when it will actually depreciate (decrease in value) over time rather than appreciate (increase in value like a home). Another mistake many people make is buying too nice of a car for their real needs when just an average car will do, or buying a new car when a less expensive used car will suffice. To keep up appearances at work and among friends, they finance their car to the hilt. Not only does this result in a higher monthly payment (which means less money is available for saving or investing), but in the end, they are still buying a depreciating asset. In fact, on average, a new car loses 17% of its value the instant you drive it off the lot. A shiny new car is undeniably appealing, but it's a far better tactic for your financial health to buy a reliable used car with cash. Doing so will help you avoid paying more than you should in interest. If you absolutely need to rely on a car loan, only buy what you can afford, and keep your credit score healthy so you can qualify for the best rates (for more advice on this, see Chapter 2: Using Credit Wisely). There are other types of "good" debt, including business loans that can help you establish or grow a business that generates revenue, but we won't get into those here.

So what kind of debt is never good debt? Personal debt, like credit card debt and other forms of unsecured debt that have no asset to back them up.

Credit Cards: A Double-Edged Sword

We explored responsible use of credit cards in Chapter 2 and the many benefits you can derive from them – perks, points, and a chance to build a healthy credit score. Now it's time to look at the downsides of credit cards.

Credit cards are what some would call "incredibly usurious," and for good reason. While many credit cards offer low introductory "teaser" rates, most credit cards carry astronomically high interest rates: 17%, 24%, even as high as 29%. Those rates don't matter if you pay off your balance in full each month, but miss one payment and you could be in the hole for quite a long time. As Benjamin Franklin noted about credit in *Poor Richard's Almanack* in 1732, "Many a man thinks he is buying pleasure when he is really selling himself a slave to it."

As we saw earlier, compounding is an incredibly powerful force that can be a huge benefit to your financial health and well-being. But it has a dark side as well. While investing money allows you to benefit from the effect of compounding interest over time, credit card interest rates are the sinister side of compounding. As the interest charges on missed payments compound every month, the inability to pay your balance in full will force you deeper and deeper into debt and can take an incredibly long time to pay off.

For instance, I use a business credit card for nearly all business expenses related to the creative agencies I run. The card has an annual percentage rate (APR) of 18.74%, which I never have to worry about thanks to an automatic payment for the full balance every single month. But if I were hypothetically only able to pay the minimum $100 every month, this APR would compound and cause my payments to balloon. American Express advertises an APR of 18.74%, but thanks to compounding, the effective interest rate making minimum payments on my current balance would be 29%, and it would take 46 months to pay off. That's almost 4 years of debt.

There's another way of thinking about this: if I were to make minimum payments instead of paying the balance off in full, not only would I be going into debt, but every single purchase I made with my credit card just became 29% more expensive. We love when items go on sale at our favorite store, but would you even consider buying something if there was a bright red sticker on it saying *NOW 30% MORE EXPENSIVE*? Not a chance. And yet, when we choose to make a minimum payment on a credit card, that's effectively what we're doing.

When you boil it down to first principles, it's not really that complicated: credit card debt of any form, in any amount is never a good thing. This is why Dave Ramsey says that "responsible use of credit does not exist" – he's speaking to people whose lives have been destroyed by exorbitantly high interest rates on their credit card debt. Yes, sometimes you have to rely on credit to tide you over in a pinch, but that's why you should have savings to cover such credit use in the first place (see Chapter 3).

To maintain a clean financial bill of health, there are a few (intentionally simple) rules when it comes to credit card debt:

1. If you don't have savings, you should not have or use a credit card. Period.
2. If you cannot pay off the balance of your credit card in full every single month without exception, cut it up and throw it away.

3. If you have any credit card debt at all, you should forego all savings and investments and make your #1 exclusive goal the elimination of this debt as soon as possible.

Minimize the Bad Debt, Manage the Good

In an ideal world, we wouldn't take on any debt at all. We would be able to pay for our homes, vehicles, education, and everything necessary for running our businesses out of pocket rather than relying on credit to help us through. But the world we inhabit looks like nothing of the sort. Homes, cars, and education are increasingly expensive, and often incomes haven't kept up with the rising price of everyday items and our conspicuous consumption.

So we need to rely on credit and debt to provide for the essentials. The golden rule of debt is to not take on any debt if you can help it. If you must, take on good debt when necessary and manage it properly (to provide a roof over your head, to educate yourself and your children, and to make sure the essentials are taken care of), but avoid bad debt at all costs.

Bad debt, such as credit card debt and other personal debt, is hands-down the best way to become a financial slave. This slavery can happen suddenly because of genuine emergencies or incrementally if we don't monitor lifestyle inflation. The credit card companies couldn't care less – they want you to become enslaved to their high interest rates. They entice you keep you entrapped for life. But chances are you have a different vision for your life, so you should do your best to avoid credit card debt at all costs.

Debt Consolidation

Many people drowning in credit card debt or student loans see ads for debt consolidation and get curious about this possible solution. But debt consolidation, which promises a lower monthly payment by combining various loans into one payment to one lender, is rarely a good idea for anyone but the lenders. Most debt consolidation plans come with extended repayment terms, which mean that you'll be in debt longer than you would have been before consolidation.

One of the main benefits of debt consolidation should be breathing room, a chance to get ahead. But to the extent that you don't change your habits, even conveniences like lower payments through debt consolidation won't do a thing for you. Also, if debt consolidation turns any of your unsecured debt into secured debt, you could be putting financial assets at risk if you fall behind on your payments.

Debt consolidation will almost always have an effect on your credit score as well. This is often due to the "age of credit" factor of your credit report we examined in Chapter 2 – consolidating your debt will lead to the elimination of older accounts, the addition of a very new account, and a significant drop in your credit score. Further, in order to save any money from debt consolidation, you'll need to pay off your balance very quickly (to take advantage of low introductory rates, etc) – but there are often penalties for pre-payment. Still further, if you were able to pay off your debt quickly, you likely wouldn't be looking into consolidation in the first place.

So while it seems tempting, debt consolidation is usually a bad idea. Just formulate a plan for repaying debt and stick to it.

Debt Repayment: Formulating a Plan

If you find yourself in debt, formulating a plan for rapid repayment should be your #1 priority. The most common and most effective debt repayment strategy is called the "Snowball Method."

Different debts have different interest rates: your student loans may only have an APR of 4.5%, but your credit card may have a rate of 19% or more. The higher the interest rate, the more money this debt will cost you...and the longer it sits there, the higher the balances will become, until the monthly payments you can afford won't even cover the interest on your loan, let alone the principal.

The Snowball Method asserts that you should pay down your highest interest rate balances first to keep this debt from spiraling out of control. This is a great strategy, and can be applied to all sorts of debt, from credit cards to student loans.

Using the Snowball Method, focus on completely eliminating your highest interest rate loan first before moving on to the next-highest rate loan. Continue making payments on the rest of your loans – usually the bare minimum – until the highest interest rate loan is 100% paid off. Then shift focus in your next-highest interest rate loan, then the next-highest, and so on.

Combine the Snowball Method with the budgeting skills you learned in Chapter 6 to pay off your balances quickly. Rather than making savings or discretionary spending a line-item in your budget, replace these categories with debt repayment – and make them as large as you can possibly afford. You can do this by ruthlessly eliminating everything that is not essential. If it's not directly related to the roof over your head, the food in your stomach, or the ability to perform your job, throw it out of your budget until all of your debt is paid off. If you use your budgeting skills to live a minimalist lifestyle for a time and become ruthless in your pursuit of debt elimination now, you will thank yourself later: the pain will eventually come to an end, and your future self will gain more financial flexibility.

Debt repayment is painful. It's supposed to be. Experience the pain of skimping on everything that you like spending money on for a few months to focus on debt repayment instead, and you'll think twice before hastily whipping out your credit card in the future. It's a painful lesson, but one that is best learned early on in life.

Other Debt Repayment Strategies

Psychologically speaking, not all academics agree that the Snow-ball Method is the most effective form of debt repayment. While tackling high interest rates is certainly the most cost-effective strategy (and the one I recommend), there is an additional burden imposed on your psyche when you feel like you're not making any progress on your loans.

Researchers from Duke University, Washington University of St. Louis, and the University of Michigan suggest that many Americans are victims of what they call "debt account aversion" – thinking about our debts is overwhelming, and we seek a sense of progress as we move towards our goal. Without any tangible measure of progress, we're unlikely to be motivated to achieve our goals. Because of this, most people tend to pay off the smallest loan first to reduce the total number of loans they have outstanding, which leads to a tangible sense of progress toward debt repayment, yet does not eliminate your biggest financial burden.

While this is not our recommended approach (as it will cost

you more in the long run), anything that gets you started down the path of debt repayment is a step in the right direction.

Debt Tolerance

By now we've seen that not all debt is created equal: some types of debt are worse than others. Likewise, not all people are created equal in this regard, and some people have higher debt tolerance levels than others. Some like to use credit cards to pay for everything, while others are more cautious – even nervous – about the possibility of being enslaved by any kind of debt whatsoever.

This probably isn't surprising to you. You may know of people who put everything on a credit card to earn points or miles, while others may prefer to use hard assets like cash to pay for everything. Our tolerance to debt dictates our behavior in many ways: some people don't mind having a car loan or lease if it means they can get a new car every two years. Others, while they could technically afford it, prefer not to carry these balances and choose instead to drive used cars bought with cash.

There isn't necessarily a right or wrong way to go about this, but it is important to (carefully) learn how much debt tolerance you have. For instance, upon graduation my wife decided that she didn't want to live in debt at all – she wanted to pay down her student loans as quickly as possible. As a result, we devised a plan to pay for all of our expenses out of my income and put 100% of her paychecks towards paying off her student loans. By doing this, she was able to pay off all of her student debt – more than $25,000 in loans – in just 11 months. This was all her: she worked incredibly hard to pursue this goal, and was able to reap the rewards of her labor. Although I offered to help, she wanted the satisfaction of paying for college by herself, and I applaud her for it. We have been incredibly blessed by the opportunity to repay debt so quickly, and I'm thankful for it – as a result of the opportunities we have been given and the hard work we've done, we can proudly say that at 25 and 22 years of age, respectively, we are 100% debt-free.

If we had a different debt tolerance, our story might be different. I have good friends who have paid off their highest interest loans and are comfortable making the minimum payments on their interest free loans in perpetuity. This means they will technically be "in debt" for the next 10 years, but doing so will enable them to take what's left over and do other things, like buy a house, save for a once-in-a-lifetime trip, or invest the difference. When you're dealing with any interest-free loan, there is always an opportunity cost to paying off debt so quickly as we did. On the other hand, there's an opportunity cost to delaying total repayment until much later.

Everybody has a different story and a different debt tolerance, and there's no one right way to address this issue – you just need to find your tolerance level and act accordingly. I believe that fast debt repayment was the right decision for my wife and me: 11 months of my wife's hard work now gives us more financial options in the future. We now get to more freely choose where our money goes and prioritize what's important to us – 100% guilt-free. We have chosen to invest and are actively saving for future goals, like buying a house someday. We both love to travel, and we can now do so freely without worrying about the bills stacking up. For instance, we are currently planning a six-month trip around the world beginning in 2019. We're planning to travel to over twenty countries, literally circling the planet once.

If we were drowning in debt, there's no way we would be able to afford this once-in-a-lifetime experience.

Depending on your debt tolerance and repayment plan, your decision will vary, but having a plan for repaying any debt you do have is the first step toward financial freedom.

Before You Move On: Make a Plan to Deal with Your Debt

If you have any credit card debt, make this your #1 priority. Student debt can be paid off in a structured way with a payment plan, but if you have any personal debt you should stop any other financial activities like investing until you've paid it off in full.

As we mentioned before, to maintain a clean financial bill of health, there are a few intentionally simple rules when it comes to credit cards and personal debt. If your financial house isn't in shape, follow these rules (in order) to get back on track:

1. If you don't have savings, you should not have or use a credit card. Period.
2. If you cannot pay off the balance of your credit card in full every single month without exception, you should consider cutting it up and throwing it away.
3. If you have any credit card debt at all, you should forego all savings and investments and make your #1 exclusive goal the elimination of this debt as soon as possible.
4. Once your credit card debt is fully paid off, focus on aggressively paying off all other forms of debt to get debt-free as soon as possible. You can resume saving and investing at this point, but I would focus on debt

elimination at the expense of other financial activities like investing.

———

NOW THAT WE'VE conquered our debt (or at least formulated a plan to effectively deal with it), we'll examine the final problem we tend to encounter with money: money myths we too easily believe.

Chapter 8

MONEY MYTHS

THE LIES WE BELIEVE ABOUT MONEY

W hen it comes to money we get into trouble in a variety of ways, but perhaps most consequential are the lies and myths we tend to believe about money. In this chapter, we'll examine 15 of the most popular myths out there, examine why each is false, and explain what we can do to have a more healthy and accurate relationship with our money.

Myth #1: Money is Evil

As we've seen, money can be a "taboo" topic. Many of us tread lightly, afraid to be viewed by our friends and family as someone who talks about money too much, for fear of being seen as obsessed. Where does this fear come from? The mistaken belief that money is evil.

Money may still be a taboo topic, but it's not evil. Money itself is morally neutral – it's a tool whose value comes from our attitudes towards it and uses for it.

Your prior experiences with money will inform your attitudes. For many in the "99%," the excesses of the rich are so off-putting that they have come to see money itself as evil. For some others who are more affluent, money seems to be the be-all end-all goal, the ultimate desire, the one thing that can seemingly solve all problems. Money, after all, can be an incredible tool for good, funding philanthropic goals or providing an education for your kids someday. Conversely, money can be a destructive tool for evil, funding drug empires and terrorism.

But in reality, money is just a tool. The Bible and other books of wisdom decry the *love* of money as the root of all evil – not money itself. So don't get caught up in believing that money itself is bad – it's what you do with it that matters.

Myth #2: Money is Safest in a Bank

You've probably heard (or believed) this myth before. If you live in America, your deposits at recognized banks are protected by the Federal Deposit Insurance Corporation (FDIC). That means the federal government will insure 100% of the money you hold at your bank, up to $250,000. If it's in the bank, you always have access to it and can't possibly lose it.

But that doesn't mean your money is truly safe. Yes, you can always get it back, but thanks to low interest rates offered by banks relative to the inflation rate, any money you have sitting in a bank account is actively getting more and more worthless the longer it sits there. Interest rates on bank accounts are almost always lower than the rate of inflation, which means that your money is gradually lowering its purchasing power over time.

"Savings accounts are the equivalent of modern-day mattress

stuffing," says Elle Kaplan, CEO of Lexion Capital Management, an asset management firm in New York City. "Savings accounts cause you to lose money over time because their low interest rates do not keep pace with inflation."

That doesn't mean you should close your savings or checking account – it just means that you should be careful about how much money you have in a bank account above and beyond what you need in the short-term to pay your bills or save for a big purchase.

Always think about the opportunity cost of where your money resides: could it be earning more elsewhere? Are there smarter places to put it? If you're looking to grow your wealth over time, the majority of your principal balance should be in investment accounts where rates of return will stay ahead of inflation. Otherwise, you're not really getting ahead.

Myth #3: Gold is a Great Investment

Gold is attractive to investors for many reasons, not least of which is its brilliant color. But is it always a good investment? Gold may seem safe – and can indeed act as a hedge against volatility in the stock market – but it may not be worth its weight.

Remember that graph from Chapter 4 showing the rates of return on different asset classes over time? Historically, gold has a real return (adjusted for inflation) of 0.7% per year – not even close to the 6.8% that stocks provide. Gold can also be highly volatile, depending on global macroeconomic conditions and how other people trade in and out of their positions.

If you're looking to build wealth for the long term, gold may make up a small percentage of your portfolio, but don't put too much stock in it. Look to other investments instead.

Myth #4: The More Money I Have, the Less I'll Think About Money

This is one of the most pervasive myths out there. Conventional wisdom would have us believe that the more money we have, the less we'll think about it. But that's simply not true.

Jeffrey Pfeffer, a professor of organizational behavior at Stanford Graduate School of Business, has studied our attitudes towards money and compensation. He found that the more money someone is paid for each hour of work they perform, the more important that money becomes. And sadly, because our compensation is so strongly tied to our feelings of self-esteem and self-worth, most of us can rarely get enough: the more money we receive, the more we need, and the greater our focus on it.

A survey of 800 people with a net worth of at least $500,000 found that 1 out of 5 of them agreed with the statement "Having enough money is a constant worry in my life." But something surprising happened when those conducting the survey asked the same question to people whose net worth was more than $10 million: 1 out of 3 of them felt that money was a constant worry in their life. Worry increased as net worth increased.

So regardless of how much money you have, you'll probably always want more. But more money may not do much more for you. That brings us to an important question: is there an ideal level of compensation for our happiness? What income is best for our satisfaction?

Myth #5: Money Can Buy Happiness

Deep down, we all know this one to be a myth: money can't really buy happiness. And yet, our attitudes and actions show our true character and lead us to believe that it can.

Research has shown that a salary of $75,000 per year was the tipping point for contentment and satisfaction. Above this level is what economists would call a "diminishing marginal utility" to each additional dollar you receive. "After you reach that amount, making more money won't substantially improve your quality of life," says Susan Bradley, a Certified Financial Planner. Our brains still betray us: regardless of compensation, most people still have a desire for more. But above $75,000 per year, our compensation has little effect on our happiness and satisfaction.

There's also significant research to show that *what* you spend your money on – not just how much you are paid – influences your happiness, too. According to Cornell psychology professor Thomas Gilovich, who has spent decades researching how our purchases affect our happiness, spending money on experiences rather than things "provides more enduring happiness."

Myth #6: Paying with Cash is Best

You probably know someone who hates credit cards and refuses to use them, preferring instead to pay with everything in cash. That may be fine for them, but it could mean they're missing out on huge benefits of responsible credit use.

Not only do you miss out on perks like cash back or rewards points by paying in cash, but you have no recourse if something goes wrong. Many credit cards offer fraud prevention, additional insurance on travel-related expenses, or extended warranties.

If you have a problem using credit cards responsibly, by all means, keep paying with cash. But if you are able to spend within your means, using cash over a credit card could be costing you in more ways than one.

MYTH #7: NEVER RENT WHEN YOU CAN OWN

Here's a controversial myth: never rent a home when you can own it instead. I tend to favor homeownership over renting, but there's an argument to be made for renting, depending on your financial goals.

It all depends on your situation: renting can be better at times, and home values don't always increase. Renting provides more flexibility, as you can move quickly. If you own a home and need to move, you could be stuck with mortgage payments if your home is slow to sell. Homeownership also comes with many costs that renting does not. You have to pay property taxes and insurance, and if a part of your home needs repair, it's up to you to fix it.

By the way, if you happen to come into a large sum of money at some point in your life, don't be too quick to pay off your mortgage. If you're not planning on living in your home for the rest of your life, you could be throwing that money away. Prepayment of a mortgage can save you money over the long run (providing there are no prepayment penalties), but again, the opportunity cost of this large sum of money is fairly high: what else could you be doing with it? If you have 15 years left on your mortgage but an investment in the stock market will on average double roughly every 10 years, might that be a better choice?

As always, it depends on your financial situation and your

goals. Just be sure to think about which situation is right for you in your stage of life.

MYTH #8: ALL DEBT IS BAD

We've already explored this myth in Chapter 7, but it's worth examining again. Many forms of personal debt, like credit card debt, are never a good thing. But others, like student loans or a mortgage, can be beneficial because they are supporting an asset (i.e. your education and future earning potential or a home) that should grow in value over time. In these cases when debt is used to fund an investment in an asset that will grow in value, the benefits typically outweigh the costs. Focus on eliminating bad debt or never taking it on in the first place while wisely managing good debt, and you should be fine.

MYTH #9: INVEST IN WHAT YOU KNOW

Putting too large of a chunk of your investment portfolio in what you know – especially if that is stock in the company you work for – is a very risky investment decision. And yet, so many Americans do it.

Take Enron, for example. The hubris that came from the company had many employees maxing out their 401(k) accounts with Enron stock just days before Enron's collapse. Most employees failed to diversify and thus exposed themselves to not one risk, but two: not only did they lose their jobs in the scandal and bankruptcy, but their retirement portfolios, which were heavily comprised of Enron stock, were decimated.

Such an investment strategy puts too many eggs in one basket and heightens your risk. A better strategy is to buy low-cost index funds that track the entire market. When you buy "total market" funds like these, you can be agnostic about most financial news. A stock shot up 15% on a surprise announcement? You don't have to feel bad about "missing out," because thanks to the index fund, you own that stock. A company announced a round of layoffs and their stock took a hit? No reason to worry – although you own that stock through your total market fund, your risk is hedged because you own the rest of the market, too.

Just because you "know" a lot about a company or have experience with their products or services because you have worked there doesn't mean it's a smart idea to put a large chunk of your portfolio in their stock. Sure, you can own some shares, but hedge your bet by buying mostly total market index funds and watch your money grow.

Myth #10: It's Not Worth Saving if I Can Only Contribute a Small Amount

This is a pervasive myth about money, especially among younger generations. As we've seen in this book, starting early does matter, regardless of the amount you're saving or investing. Maybe you're not in a position to save 10% of your income. Maybe you can't even set aside 5%. That's ok. Just take whatever amount you are able and set it aside. By doing so, you will be leveraging the most important asset you have at your disposal: time.

Over time, you can increase this amount as you are able, and you should see more significant returns from it. It will feel like you're getting somewhere. You can always earn more and contribute more money to your investments, but you can never go back to replace lost time. The dollar amount, however small, doesn't matter. Just start now.

MYTH #11: I'M YOUNG – I DON'T NEED TO START SAVING FOR RETIREMENT NOW

A corollary to Myth #10 is the belief that you don't need to start saving for retirement until you're older. Wrong. Granted, it can be tough to find extra money to invest and save when you're just starting out. But as we discovered with Myth #10, the important thing is to start now to reap the rewards of compounding.

Later on, you'll have even more expenses: a spouse, a mortgage, maybe even a few kids to feed and educate, or aging parents to care for. Although it may seem like life is expensive now, it gets even more expensive later – and later on, you won't have as much time to prepare for retirement. By starting now, regardless of age or how much you're able to save, your future self will thank you. Again, as Warren Buffett has said, "Someone's sitting in the shade today because someone planted a tree a long time ago." So just start now.

MYTH #12: THE STOCK MARKET IS RISKY

This myth spans nearly every age group, demographic, ethnicity, and nationality on earth: many people believe the stock market is risky, even incredibly risky, and one should not therefore place their hard-earned money in it. But this couldn't be further from the truth.

Yes, there is risk of loss associated with any investment, regardless of what you're investing in. But when you embrace a long-term investment horizon, the stock market is not as risky as many would have us believe. Let's again be reminded about what has happened to the American stock market from 1900 until the present day: in the last 118 years, the United States endured two world wars and other traumatic and expensive military conflicts, the Great Depression, more than a dozen recessions and financial panics, oil shocks, corporate collapses, disgraced presidencies, the Great Recession, widening wage gaps, and more. And yet the Dow rose from 66 to 24,274. That's a 36,678% increase.

While nobody actually lives long enough to capture this sort of return, the math is simple: the stock market has proven to consistently grow over time. As Benjamin Graham, the mentor to Warren Buffett, said long ago, "In the short term, the stock market is a voting machine. But in the long term, it's a weighing machine."

Yes, there will be temporary volatility and price changes in any market. As Nobel laureate Daniel Kahneman discovered, we suffer from "recency bias" – we tend to weight more recent events more heavily in our memory. So when the ticker tape flashes red across the bottom of CNBC, we tend to believe that the stock market is "risky." But when you start investing at a young age and seek to build lasting wealth for the long term, the risk is significantly mitigated.

MYTH #13: THERE'S NO WAY OF KNOWING HOW MUCH MONEY I'LL NEED FOR RETIREMENT

If you were to ask 100 people about retirement and how much money they thought they would need, you'd probably get 100 answers...if everybody was able to answer at all, that is.

Retirement mystifies people. Traditionally, it was common to work forty years or more at one organization, get a gold watch, and retire at 65. But many features of our economy have changed: we switch jobs – or careers, for that matter – much more often, and more and more people are choosing to retire later than 65. This is often times by necessity. It's pretty likely that your lifestyle will change dramatically between the ages of 25 and 65, so it may be hard to picture how you'll live in retirement or how much money will be required. In fact, it is estimated that the average twenty-something will change careers – not just jobs, but careers – four to seven times over their working life. Many jobs we will one day hold have not been invented yet.

Estimating how much money we'll need for retirement can be complicated and will vary depending on our financial situation, cost of living, career choices made, and the lifestyle we aspire to live. But knowing how much money we'll need doesn't have to be rocket science.

Investment firm Fidelity did the math and came up with some guidelines that should help you in your calculations. They recommend saving at least 15% of your pretax income every year, including employer contributions. To see if you're on track, use a basic rule of thumb for retirement savings: Aim to have saved at least 1x your income at age 30, 3x at age 40, 7x at age 55, and 10x by age 67. Of course, everyone's situation is unique and you may find that you need to save more or less than this suggested guideline.

Experts recommend that you withdraw no more than 4% of your portfolio's balance per year in retirement. If you expect to retire later, live longer, or spend more, you will need to adjust your formula accordingly. So, if you have $500,000 in retirement savings, they suggest to withdraw no more than $20,000 annually.

There are a number of robust retirement calculators online,

including some that factor in other sources of income, such as how much Social Security you're likely to receive at retirement. For a complete list, visit www.moneyformillennialsbook.com.

MYTH #14: ACTIVE INVESTMENT FUNDS OUTPERFORM INDEX FUNDS

Another popular myth is that actively-traded investments outperform "boring" investments like index funds, but this couldn't be further from the truth. Actively trading in and out of positions has two main drawbacks: for one, active trading triggers capital gains taxes more frequently (and any positions held under one year are subject to a much higher short term capital gains tax). The other downside of active trading is commissions: if you have money with an active money manager, their active investment strategy results in you paying them more in commissions and fees, which eat away at your profits.

A confident believer in the power of index funds that match the market, Warren Buffett made a famous bet in 2008 with active fund manager Ted Seides. Buffett bet $1 million that including fees, costs, and expenses, an S&P 500 index fund would outperform a hand-picked portfolio of actively-traded hedge funds over a 10-year time period. Buffett appeared to "lose" money early as the market tanked in 2008, because the hedge funds lost less since they were "hedged" against the risk of downturn. However, the index fund took the lead in later years, and at the end of the bet, a clear winner emerged: Buffett's index funds had gained 7.1% per year for the past 10 years, compared to 2.2% per year for the hedge fund. As a result, Buffett donated the $1 million in winnings to the Boys and Girls Club of Omaha.

Not only do actively-traded funds make mistakes and lose money to capital gains taxes, but their expenses and fees are far higher, which eats into profits in a way that index funds never will. If you want to build long-term wealth, adopt a long-term mindset, invest passively, and watch the money grow.

MYTH #15: YOU CAN TIME THE STOCK MARKET

The final myth we'll look at is the belief that you can "time" the market to take advantage of anomalies in business value by using *technical analysis,* which seeks to forecast the direction of prices through the study of past market data, primarily price and volume of trading.

But this approach doesn't work. The market has so many millions of participants that any material change in the underlying value of the business is reflected by the price nearly instantly. The stock market moves seemingly at random, so you don't have much of a chance of trading in and out of positions so quickly that you only make money and never lose money. There aren't any secrets contained in the chart of a stock, nor can you lock in certain gains with any "pattern" you see. Our brains love to think that we can recognize and interpret patterns to profit from them, but when it comes to the randomness of the stock market, it's a great way to get burned. Most honest stock brokers will tell you that it is extremely difficult to beat the major indices.

The best bet is to buy stocks and hold them for the long run. Even better, buy an entire "basket" of securities by purchasing a total stock market index fund, hold it, and watch it grow. If you try to time the market, you'll only end up losing money due to poor timing, poor decisions, and capital gains from active trading. It really is best to just buy and hold the entire market.

———

Now that we've taken a look at the myths and lies most people tend to believe about money, we turn our attention to a chief aim of aspiring investors of all ages: how to build passive income, automate your financial life, and make your money work for you.

PART III

OUR ASPIRATIONS
FOR MONEY

Chapter 9

MAKING MONEY WORK FOR YOU

AUTOMATE YOUR FINANCES TO REACH
FINANCIAL INDEPENDENCE FASTER

R egardless of where you find yourself at the moment, chances are you might like to change things up a bit. Whether you are absolutely in love with your job or dread the thought of spending another second in your current position, you probably wouldn't argue against a little more financial freedom: the ability to set your own hours, spend more time on passion projects, learn new skills, or travel more. This is a fairly common desire regardless of our season of life or our financial situation, but it is particularly acute with our generation. Especially as the demands on our time increase in our 24/7, "always-on" world, we could all use a bit more time, flexibility, and variance in our days.

Such a flexible lifestyle seems achievable only to the rich, but it's actually more accessible to ordinary folks than you would think. The democratization of work through the so-called "gig economy," combined with the free flow of information on the Internet and an abundance of relatively cheap capital means that we can increasingly choose the lifestyle we want to live and the work habits we want to adopt. While opportunities may seem scarce, there has never been a better time to develop the skills necessary to free yourself from a traditional 9-5 schedule or the demands of the corporate world. It takes hard work, but I believe that there are still ample opportunities to earn money and build a satisfying career on your terms. Our grandparents' model of working forty years for one company and getting a gold watch when you retire is dead.

This so-called "lifestyle design" has been popularized by books such as *The 4-Hour Workweek* by Tim Ferriss, and it's appealing for a reason: if you didn't have to spend eight hours a day chained to a desk in order to make ends meet, would you? Many of us would say no. If money was no object and we could design our ideal lifestyle, we'd spend more time learning new skills, traveling to new places, or spending time on things that make us feel alive. We would pursue our dreams. We would build companies. We would spend more quality time with our families. We would feel as though we had finally been given permission to thrive, and we'd love it.

But that's the problem: money, or rather the lack of it, often *is* an object that gets in our way. We need money to survive and provide for our families. And so we get up each weekday morning, clock in, and get to work. The nature of work may be changing, but for many of us, we still have to go to work each and every day to earn a living.

I'm not suggesting that work is a bad thing. In fact, just the opposite: work can be incredibly fulfilling, meaningful, and can improve both the lives of those whom your work serves and your life as well. But I am suggesting that a little more flexibility in the relationships we have with our jobs could be a good thing. If we didn't have to spend all of our "working lives" actually at work, we could take advantage of so many other opportunities. We would be free to explore other interests, meet new people, and exercise our inner creative capacity to a greater extent than our hectic work schedules currently allow.

Sounds like a pipe dream or a lofty ambition, right? It's not. But even if we aren't able to *fully* attain this goal, let's explore how we can introduce more freedom and margin into our working lives.

The Difference Between the Poor, Middle Class, and the Rich

There's a phenomenon that's on the rise around the world: an increasingly large gap between the upper class and everyone else. Although capitalistic societies like America's seem to exacerbate the issue, this problem is universal in nature. It spans across continents, ethnicities, and financial markets, affecting nearly everyone the world over. Slice and dice the data however you want – the numbers don't lie. Those in the upper classes of society are getting overwhelmingly wealthier, while the poor and middle class seem to be getting left behind. Income disparity and capitalism combined with democracy are highly correlated for obvious reasons.

Because of this growing wealth- and income-inequality gap, discussions of "Universal Basic Income" (UBI) are on the rise, with proponents from economists to Silicon Valley elites singing its praises (Chris Hughes, a co-founder of Facebook, is a vocal supporter). UBI would guarantee all citizens a set amount of money on a monthly basis, regardless of whether they worked or not. It's money for nothing.

Let me be clear: this is not what I'm advocating when I refer to the desire to "design your lifestyle" or to "make your money work for you." I do not think UBI is a viable option, nor do I find it a beneficial solution to our income inequality problems. There are lots of issues with UBI, not the least of which is disincentivizing productive work and contribution to society and the loss of dignity that comes from working to provide for your family, but I won't get into those here. If you're interested in wealth inequality, a fascinating book to read is *The Price of Inequality* by Joseph Stiglitz.

Debates about wealth inequality and a growing income gap aside, the increasing gap between rich and poor is a rather simple one to explain. It boils down to one simple issue: what we do with our money – what we buy and consume. The most basic explanation of wealth inequality is fairly simple: the poor tend to buy liabilities, the middle class tends to buy goods, and those in the upper class tend to buy assets. This is not a hard-and-fast rule – to some extent, people in every socioeconomic class will have some assets, some goods, and some liabilities. Rather, this is a simple heuristic that can help you and me understand this issue and give us actionable steps to take should we want to improve our lot in life. Let me explain what I mean here.

On average, those in the lower class tend to buy *liabilities* – those items whose use and consumption costs more than they are worth in and of themselves. Rather than being items that grow your net worth and expand the options available to you, liabilities are things that take money out of your pockets. Examples of liabilities the lower class tends to acquire include cars (which tend to have expensive monthly payments, insurance, and depreciation costs), mobile homes (which act much more like a car than a home, depreciating rather than growing in value), lottery tickets (your odds of getting struck by lightning are higher than winning most lotteries), payday loans with exorbitantly high interest rates, and other miscellaneous consumables (food, alcohol, cigarettes, drugs, etc).

Acquisition of liabilities can be due to many factors, including small and stagnant incomes. The poor are not entirely "at fault" for many of these purchases, often because they have no other viable option. If you were struggling to make ends meet with a meager income and had to get a payday loan to make rent, provide shelter for your family, and put food on the table, wouldn't you? If it was the only option available, I know I would.

Many items that could be seen as "assets" are more expensive, and therefore out of reach to those occupying lower income brackets. But as I said, this is not a hard-and-fast rule, and there are still possibilities for upward mobility among those in lower income brackets. Whether by choice or by necessity, the poor tend to buy liabilities, and it's hindering their ability to move ahead.

The middle class, on the other hand, tend to buy *goods* – things that do not necessarily decrease their standard of living or act as a liability, but do not contribute to a growing net worth either. The middle class may have some assets, like a home, and they may have some liabilities that drag them down, but on the whole much of their purchasing behavior is targeted at goods indented for consumption. Our economy is built upon 70% consumable items.

Surprisingly, middle class consumption may include some liabilities that are pretending to be assets, including certificates of deposit (CDs), bonds, and some (though not all) real estate purchases. That seems wrong at first: how can CDs, bonds, or real estate actually be a liability? Let's look at an example.

For simplicity, let's assume a middle class person buys a $1000 CD. In exchange for their $1000, the bank promises to repay the depositor a return of 3% on their money for a 1-year term (which is higher than the current rate, by the way) – at the end of a year, the bank will return $1030. Seems like a gain, right? Well, if you're in the 15% tax bracket, you'll have to pay 15% on your earnings ($4.50), reducing your net profit to $25.50. But thanks to inflation (let's assume 3%), the purchasing power of both the $1000 you "invested" *and* the $25.50 of profit have each decreased. So after a year of loaning out your $1000, you now have purchasing power of $970 + $24.74, for a grand total of $994.74. You've actually lost money, so what you thought was an asset has turned out to be a liability.

Residential real estate that you actually live in can also be a short-term liability that masquerades as an asset. Homeownership is often considered "America's best investment," but when you think about it, owning a home has many externalities and costs associated with it. We hope to make money when we sell our home, but it's never a sure thing. Beyond the taxes, insurance, and home repairs, our mortgage is the obvious big expense that comes with homeownership. Let's say you get a mortgage from your bank at 6%. You'll get a deduction for the interest you pay on your mortgage (up to $10,000 under current tax law). If you're in the 15% tax bracket, this effectively lowers your mortgage rate to 5.1%. Generally your house will appreciate over time, somewhere around the rate of inflation (although the actual appreciation rate may be greater or less, depending on a variety of factors). By the time you're done paying for insurance, property taxes, and upkeep, you'll probably break even...so it's not technically a liability, but it may not be the best-performing asset, either.

From an investment perspective, homeownership has two main advantages: it is essentially a forced savings plan (you wouldn't want to skip out on paying your mortgage). It's also fairly difficult to dip into the equity you've built up in your home, although home equity loans are making this easier. So depending on a variety of factors, your home may be a good investment over the long term, although it can often function as a short-term liability. The real enemy when considering wealth-building assets is inflation, the erosion of your purchasing power over time. Inflation has an effect on nearly all types of "investments," and inflation rates and taxes should always be taken into account when making investment decisions.

Unlike the ownership and purchasing habits of the poor and middle class, the rich are in a completely different situation. Yes, to some extent everybody has some assets and some liabilities, but the rich tend to acquire more *assets* than those in the lower and middle classes (and fewer liabilities). Examples of such assets include second or third homes, sizable positions in the stock market (well-diversified positions that include many total stock market funds, of course), stock options in companies they run or control, or even money at exclusive institutions such as hedge funds.

These opportunities are not available or affordable for everyone, but these assets are a huge way that the rich see their net worth grow at a faster rate than the rest of society. For example, thanks to a the rapid growth of Amazon, the company's CEO Jeff Bezos has become the wealthiest person on the face of the planet. In fact, Bezos saw his net worth increase by $40 *billion* in the first six months of 2018 alone. This is of course an extreme example, but thanks to their accumulation of financial assets the wealth of the rich has an opportunity to increase each and every day.

Differences in Mindset

Another main difference between the upper class and the rest of us is mindset. While many of us tend to think of ownership in terms of dollar amount, the upper class tend to view ownership in terms of cash flows. Let's say a wealthy person wants to buy a luxury car like a Mercedes-Benz. She has the cash in the bank, but will she go buy the car for cash? Maybe not. Instead, she may identify an investment that can give her a decent return – let's say a stock that pays out a 5% dividend. Thanks to a great credit score, she can then go finance a new Mercedes at, say, a 3.5% APR. She will then use the cash generated by the yearly dividend from the equity she just purchased to essentially pay for her monthly car payment. In fact, with this "interest arbitrage," she will make some extra each month as well (this example ignores the tax collected on the dividend for simple math, but you get the idea). So there you have it: a brand new luxury car and some profit thrown in for good measure. Sounds nice, doesn't it?

This is a key habit those in the upper class often take advantage of: they finance their lifestyle with interest from their invest-ments *without ever touching the principal.* Their money stays safe and can grow in value over time, and the interest they are paid for investing can finance the lifestyle they want to lead.

This principle translates to the real estate holdings of the upper class as well. Often times, the rich buy income-producing real estate, like commercial office space, residential real estate that can be rented out, or self-storage facilities to house the "stuff" those in the middle and lower classes acquire. Let's say they receive a 5% or 6% return on these investments. While this may seem like a paltry sum compared to higher returns the stock market may pay out, there's a key difference: with investments in the stock market, you have to put up 100% of your own money. With real estate, most of the investment is financed. You may contribute 20% for a down payment while you (or rather, your tenants) finance the rest. *They* pay off the principal and retire your debt while *you* get wonderful tax deductions and own more and more of the asset with each passing year.

These habits and practices are not an exception for the upper class, but the norm. Ownership of assets gives the rich leverage on a scale that those in lower classes simply don't have access to. But that doesn't mean those with lower incomes can't replicate the practices of the rich on a smaller scale. Everybody has equal opportunity in a capitalistic society. What we are not promised is equal outcomes. We may not own a home in the Hamptons, but we can use our home as an asset – or even better, buy a second home as a rental property that produces residual income. If you want to mimic the returns the mega-wealthy realize – on whatever scale – there are a number of opportunities to do so.

Financial Independence

There's a huge movement around "financial independence" these days (sometimes called "early retirement"). Financial independence is what we've just discussed: the ability to design the lifestyle you want without having to rely 100% on a traditional 9-to-5 work schedule...or take a paycheck at all for that matter. Reaching a state of financial independence means that you can live off of investment returns and never have to rely on a bi-weekly paycheck to finance your lifestyle.

Achieving such a feat depends on a number of factors, including how much you earn, what your monthly or yearly expenses are, and other life factors (Are you getting married soon?

Expecting to have a child?). Everybody has a number. *What's yours?*

To calculate how much you would need to be "financially independent," you'll need to take a look at your monthly expenses. Similar to retirement at or around 65, we'll stick to the *4% Rule* here – you can safely withdraw up to 4% of your investment portfolio's value each year (adjusting for inflation each year as well) without compromising your principal.

To calculate how much money you'll need to let 4% finance your lifestyle, simply take your yearly expenses and multiply by 25 (25 x 4% = 100%). Some financial independence calculators will tell you to multiply your monthly expenses by 300 (25 x 12 = 300) – the math is the same. For example, if you live off a yearly budget of $50,000, you'll need $1,250,000 to "retire early." If you can manage to live off $40,000 a year, you will only need $1,000,000 to be financially independent.

This may seem like a lot, but there are ways to reach this goal faster. Cutting unnecessary expenses is the best one. Take a hard look at how much you spend compared to how much you make. The greater this ratio, the faster you'll be able to reach financial independence.

Let's look at a seemingly extreme example: let's assume you have $0 in savings, you make $50,000 a year, and thanks to a minimalist lifestyle, you're able to live off $20,000 a year. That means you're saving 60% of your income, which you are then able to invest. Thanks to life circumstances and creative budgeting, you can live on the cheap and save most of what you make (think about Brandon, the engineer at Google who lives in his truck).

What will all your hard work get you? Assuming a 6.8% annual rate of return and a withdrawal rate of 4%, you'd be able to retire in 11.5 years. I'm 26 right now, so if I was able to do this, I could "retire" (or at least design the lifestyle I want, no questions asked) at 37:

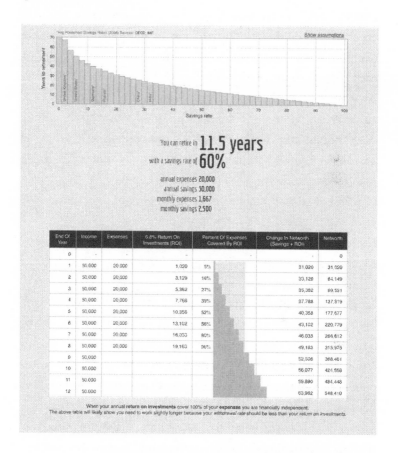

Of course, this assumes that my hypothetical $20,000-a-year expenses would stay constant, and that I'd never spend more than this even after I was financially independent. These numbers will likely change, but you get the idea: if you want to fast-track financial independence, cut spending as much as possible and focus on saving every penny that you can.

Cutting expenses is one way to achieve financial independence faster, but so is increasing income. If I only made $50,000 from a regular paycheck but started a side business earning $10,000 per year and saved all of it, I could retire in 9.6 years if expenses remained at $20,000 per year. That would mean reaching financial independence *2 years faster* – just for getting creative with income sources!

Even if you don't (or can't) follow this path of financial austerity for the long term, any period of dramatically cutting expenditures will be beneficial for your long-term financial health, as it gives you more "wiggle room." Chances are you'll find out the things in your life that you truly do need, as opposed to what's unnecessary altogether, or just "nice to have," and make some adjustments.

Is Financial Independence Right for You?

In the end, it all boils down to your financial goals. Maybe you'd like to quit your job and travel the world for a year, or maybe having an extra $500 a month would satisfy your goals. True financial freedom may not be right for everyone. But even if life circumstances don't allow you to achieve early retirement, there's nothing stopping you from earning some extra money on the side that gives you a little more margin to travel, make a big purchase, or achieve other financial goals.

Financial independence isn't – and probably shouldn't be – your ultimate goal, because the satisfaction we should derive from our work is rewarding. If you'd like to change a thing or two about your employment situation, say find a new job that more closely aligns your goals or take a job that pays less but better suits your passions, that's totally fine.

There really is something inherently rewarding about the work we do, regardless of how much we are paid for it. We've all heard stories about retirees who get so bored playing golf all day that they enter the workforce again. Although it's hard for me to imagine getting bored by such incredible levels of freedom when you're young, so many retirees fall into this predicament that the number of retirees who re-enter the workforce has reached record levels. More margin in our lives to create the careers we desire and to have enough financial flexibility to live our desired lifestyle is certainly attractive to most people, but for some, true financial independence has little to no appeal. Take my dad, for example.

My dad grew up as the second of five kids in Santa Cruz, California. His family was lower-middle class: they lived off of his dad's income and bought groceries on the 15th and the 30th of each month (when the paychecks were cut). As a family of seven, they lived in an 1,100 square foot house on a quiet cul-de-sac. His parents were high-school sweethearts who married young and never went to college. Their infrequent vacations were road trips in the family's station wagon. As a family, they were happy – they had a roof over their heads, food on the table, and their needs were taken care of. But there was very little wiggle room. When my dad was 12 years old and wanted a bike but there wasn't any money for it, he worked to buy one for himself.

Fast-forward 30 years or so, and in the early 1990s my dad started a mortgage credit reporting company, growing it from one employee (him) in an office in the back of a barn (yes, literally) to several hundred employees in less than a decade. Those were the days when applying for a mortgage meant a lengthy credit check, a process that took up to 5 business days and cost $60. Through early forms of artificial intelligence and predictive modeling, his company was able to bring the credit check process from $60 down to under $10 and from 5 days down to 60 seconds. At the height of their business, they were processing more than 10,000 mortgage applications nationwide every single day.

As a result of the technology his company pioneered, in 1996 my dad had the opportunity to sell to a Fortune 500 corporation for a large sum. At the young age of 36, with a wife and three kids, this one financial event made him financially independent. At that moment, he had more money than his parents made in their entire working lives. He never had to take a paycheck for the rest of his life if he didn't want to. For many, this was the American dream: through hard work and dedication, he was able to pull himself up from a lower-middle class childhood to levels of financial achievement most could only dream of.

And yet, he realized something: at 36, he probably had more than 50 years left to live – he couldn't spend every day for the rest of his life golfing. To him, it was a waste of his God-given gifts and passions to simply sit back and "mail it in." The money was more than he and my mom could ever need, so they gave much of it away. Growing up, we enjoyed a comfortable life – we had nice things and received a very good education, but our lifestyle wasn't what most people would think of when told to imagine the "rich." Rather, my parents saw this newfound financial freedom as an opportunity to bless other people rather than use it solely for themselves. After all, my dad still had a lot of work left in him. And so he went back to work.

At first, he went to work for the company that acquired him, becoming one of their executives and running a large division. This lasted for three years or so, until he came to another inflection point: he was offered an opportunity for even more responsibility, which included some nice perks. But he would be on the road for much of the year.

Ok, surely *this* had to be the American dream: to start a company, get acquired, and rise to the very top of the corporate ladder? Surely nothing could be better than this. So what did he do?

He said no and eventually left the company.

This astounded those who worked at the top. He was privately told by another executive who was amazed at his boldness to refuse the offer, *"Nobody ever says no to an offer like this."* Like so many publicly-traded companies, this particular company had a culture that sought to maximize profitability at all costs.

But for my dad, the choice was easy: he was simply unwilling to spend so much time away from his family, regardless of the compensation. They could throw all the money in the world at him and the answer would still be no. Financial independence wasn't the goal – certain things, like his family, were more important to him, and no amount of money was worth sacrificing those relationships.

So regardless of your situation, perhaps financial independence shouldn't be the goal; maybe a little more financial margin is a good place to start. Your goals and desires for money may be very different than others' – just set a goal and devise a plan for pursuing it.

Wiggle Room

If financial freedom isn't for you, that's ok. Maybe life circumstance dictate otherwise, or maybe you'd be content with just a little more "wiggle room." If you just want to diversify income sources and get a little extra breathing room, there are many ways to do it. As with so many other parts of your financial journey, now is the best time to begin.

Research has shown that the average millionaire has seven different sources of income. They may have a primary income that comes from a traditional career, but they don't have to be 100% dependent on it.

There are many ways to diversify your income sources, all of which exist on a spectrum from easy to difficult. On the easier end of things, there's always the option of selling things online. This can be as simple as selling handmade goods on Etsy, or engaging in "retail arbitrage" as Gary Vaynerchuk and others advocate for (basically, buying unwanted items at garage sales and re-selling them on eBay for a profit). With a little technical savvy, you can also sell your own "knowledge" products online, such as an online course or an eBook. Own a car? You can always drive for Lyft or Uber. These markets are getting saturated (and there's evidence that they don't pay that well after expenses and depreciation), but it's an option to carefully consider.

For those seeking something a little more complex, you can try selling services online rather than just goods. This includes fields such as freelancing, consulting, and selling other specialized services that fit your skillset. By doing this, you can join the rise of knowledge workers who are paid for the value of the knowledge they provide, not just the physical work they produce.

There's another path that is more difficult and requires more up-front investment, though it is not impossible. For many, the acquisition of real estate is an important part of their journey to greater levels of financial independence. Owning real estate that is rented out can help you realize financial goals faster. However, real estate generally requires a more significant up-front investment (and maybe that's a goal you could save for). More varied – and more expensive – problems can arise with real estate as opposed to selling something online, so it's not for everyone. But the benefits of owning real estate can be substantial: someone else (your tenant) is retiring your debt over time while you get to build equity in a tangible asset, and chances are you can deduct the interest you pay on your mortgage and reap the rewards on your taxes. Obviously, the best option (or options) for you will depend on your financial goals and your life circumstances. If your circumstances allow it, perhaps the best option is to pursue all three.

For instance, I have been fortunate enough to be able to participate in many of these opportunities at the age of 26. I earn most of my income from web design projects at my two agencies (my "paycheck" if you will). Another source of income comes from retainers, consulting, and technical support related to these web design projects, which includes website maintenance, SEO, and other ongoing work billed on a monthly basis. I have sold various products online, from bumper stickers on Amazon to tie clips made from bourbon barrels on Etsy (not kidding). I do some writing on Medium, which pays me depending on how many "members" enjoy and vote for my work (this amount is very small – usually under $20 per month – but everything counts). I have tried my hand at creating knowledge products online (this book is one); although most of them never went anywhere, I have learned a lot and enjoyed the process. And although my wife and I rent our one-bedroom apartment, I bought my first home as an investment property when I was 23.

The point here is not to show off – for many, buying a home or establishing a side venture isn't a means to financial achievement, but rather a way of providing for their family's current needs. That's 100% ok – regardless of your goals or financial "achievement," the point is to show you that with some creativity, it is possible to reach your goals faster than you thought possible.

————

Whatever your financial goals may be, achievement of them isn't guaranteed to make you happy. After all, the acquisition of money isn't the be-all end-all goal of life. There's significant research showing that what you *do* with your money has more of an impact on your life satisfaction and happiness than *how much* money you have in the first place. And that's why we've saved the best for last. In our final chapter, we'll explore one of the most important topics related to money: strategically and generously giving it away.

Chapter 10

PHILANTHROPY AND GIVING MONEY AWAY

YOU CAN'T TAKE IT WITH YOU, AFTER ALL

Our discussion of money and personal finance in your twenties is nearly over, but no discussion about personal finance would be complete without exploring the topic of philanthropy and giving money away. By itself, the unbridled pursuit of money is a waste. It leaves us feeling empty and dissatisfied, as if there is no meaningful purpose to life beyond our own selfish pursuits. Remember in the preface of this book when I noticed so many ultra-wealthy people in my college's community who seemed so empty, hollow, and unsatisfied with their lives? Regardless of how much money we have in our bank account, the pursuit of money for money's sake is pointless.

There is simply no straightforward relationship between wealth and well-being. Studies have shown that adults in both America and Great Britain report lower levels of life satisfaction and contentedness today then they did fifty years ago, despite an increase in living standards and material wealth. Money is merely a tool, not the goal; if we are to use our money well, we must build generosity and philanthropic giving into our belief system.

Sadly, so many people think that they cannot afford to give money away – or even to begin thinking about giving money away – until they strike it rich. Indeed, while many in our society like the idea of charitable giving, our actions betray the attitudes of our hearts (and our tight grip over our wallets): many people feel like they cannot afford to give until they're wealthy. To them, philanthropic giving is only for billionaires like Bill Gates and Oprah.

But that belief couldn't be further from the truth. Granted, it may be a challenge to give money to support charitable organizations if you're only making $20,000 per year, but most of us could find a little wiggle room in our budgets to be generous – if we wanted to, that is.

There are many reasons to give money away: one might wish to support their church or religious organization (31% of all charitable giving in 2017 was to religious organizations). They may give for the social good of their community or support a cause near and dear to their heart. Charitable giving to qualified organizations also has tax benefits. Hopefully you're not giving money away solely for the tax deduction, but lowering your tax bill can be a factor in where you choose to give, as we saw in Chapter 5.

But giving money away isn't just beneficial to those who are receiving it – surprisingly, giving money away is actually good for you. Studies have shown that the act of giving money away has positive effects on our happiness and life satisfaction. Recent research from Stanford's Graduate School of Business suggests that the most satisfying way we can use our money is to invest it in others; people derive more satisfaction spending money on others than they do spending money on themselves. Both the Bible and Stanford agree: it truly is better to give than to receive.

The effect that spending money on others has on us doesn't have to mean giving away millions of dollars, as Bill Gates, Warren Buffett, and other billionaires do. In fact, one study showed that giving as little as $1 away to someone else can cause you to feel both healthier and wealthier – maybe not in the pure financial sense of the word, but such an act helps you feel like you're living a more rich and satisfying life.

Charitable giving doesn't just make us feel warm and fuzzy in an ephemeral way, either – our brains' pleasure circuits are activated by acts of charity. Research has shown that most "transcendent experiences" in our lives – from exercise to deep learning and prayer – activate an anatomically defined "pleasure circuit" in the brain. This area of the brain is called the *medial forebrain pleasure circuit*, in which dopamine plays a crucial role. It is in these brain tissues that pleasure is felt, and it is also the medial forebrain where psychoactive substances like cocaine, nicotine, and heroin have their effect. Generosity and even volunteerism can also contribute to better physical health and increased longevity.

So it's clear that giving money away is good for us, so long as it's authentic and sincere. Yet philanthropic giving should be strategic: throwing money indiscriminately at any cause won't give you many benefits, not to mention the fact that it's not sustainable. The best giving is very strategic and well thought out. Let me explain what I mean.

As part of an Executive Leadership course I took my senior year of college, a guest lecturer came to speak to our class. He was very accomplished and had enjoyed a storied career: he worked for a major investment banking firm on Wall Street for several years and was eventually asked to open their Silicon Valley office to help find and fund the next world-changing technology firms emerging from Northern California. He funded some of the largest corporations in history. If you were to look up a list of the top 50 investment bankers in American history, this guy would be on it.

As a result of his work in taking these companies public, he came to know the CEOs fairly well. Fast-forward several years, and he asked one of these CEOs (who was one of the wealthiest people in the world) why he hadn't seriously ramped up his philanthropic work. After all, he was a billionaire, which was far more money than anyone could ever spend in one hundred lifetimes, let alone one.

The CEO's response to his question was surprising. He told our speaker that he believed effective philanthropic giving required a thoughtfulness and intensity akin to the focus required to run a major corporation. Put simply, the CEO hadn't yet thought deeply enough about where he wanted to give his money. He was thinking about it and working on it, but he just wasn't there yet. His response wasn't defensive; it wasn't an attempt to miserly hoard his billions and not give any away. Rather, he wanted to be methodical and thoughtful about where and how his money could be given to have the biggest impact. For him, to throw money at every problem or opportunity without thought would be wasteful.

I love this story because it acknowledges the difficulty imposed on the ultra-wealthy when they consider how to be philanthropic. Although it may seem unfair to say that someone as wealthy as this CEO has an incredible burden on his shoulders, I think that's accurate. If you have been blessed with the financial means to affect change on a massive scale, you have an incredible responsibility to ensure those dollars are used as effectively as possible. Anything else would be a waste. So even if you're just trying to determine how to give that extra $100 a month in your budget, it demands a thoughtful approach.

A Few Philanthropic Pointers

Everybody has different values and goals when it comes to charitable giving. Various causes resonate to certain people for different reasons. For some, tithing to their place of worship is most important; to others, social or political causes take precedence. For others still, international organizations may fit the bill. I can't advise you on what may be best for you to give your money away to, but here are a few pointers to ensure you get the most bang for your buck.

Charity Navigator

Charity Navigator (www.charitynavigator.org) is an excellent resource to use when you're doing research on charitable organizations. By using publicly-available information, they assign each non-profit with a "rating" that takes into account their financial performance, accountability, and transparency metrics so you can see where your money is going. The highest-rated charities spend very little money on administrative expenses, but devote most of the donations they receive to funding their programs and services. Another great resource for Christian giving is the National Christian Foundation.

Make Sure It's a 501(c)(3)

If you want to make sure your contributions are tax-deductible, you have to first ensure that you're giving to an accredited 501(c)(3) or similar non-profit organization. Otherwise, you won't be able to write off contributions as tax-deductible under federal law. If you're unsure about the non-profit status of an organization, Charity Navigator and other services can help you with this, but usually an organization will have a disclosure on their website.

Forget the Money – Focus on the Story

Finally, it's not about the money anyway. When you're doing research on how to give, pay attention to the story you're being told – not necessarily the story of the organization itself, but the stories of how your donations will help them perform their work and the people it will impact. Most organizations eager to get ahold of your wallet will feature stories of those whose lives have changed because of your generosity. These stories can be incredibly helpful in determining how you want to allocate dollars to charitable giving.

Learning to give hard-earned money away for the benefit of others can be a challenge. At the very least, it's a skill that should be developed and nurtured over a lifetime. Giving for the benefit of others is an important skill that has tremendous benefits for both us and society at large. With proper budgeting skills, you can both contribute to your own well-being and help others in the process, too. You may not yet be good at giving money away, or you may not feel like you're able to have the impact you desire to have yet, but please start, for your sake and for others.

JUST LIKE EVERYTHING else with personal finance, it's not the dollar amount that matters but the habit and the willingness to begin now. For instance, I'm not great at charitable giving yet, but I hope to get better over time. It's an important skill to develop, both for ourselves and others. You can be well-educated about personal finance and have all the right skills, but miss the point entirely: at the end of the day, it's not about the money anyway.

ONE LAST THING...

If you enjoyed this book, please consider leaving a review on Amazon or Goodreads – every review helps spread the word about *Money for Millennials* and gives more young people a chance to learn how to manage their finances wisely in their twenties...which, as you know by now, is the best way to build substantial long-term wealth.

Leave a review on Amazon here:
www.bit.ly/M4MAmazonReview

Leave a review on Goodreads here:
www.bit.ly/M4MGoodreadsReview

For more information and resources to help you manage your money better, including a list of the best financial tools to help in your journey, please visit **www.moneyformillennialsbook.com.**

PAY IT FORWARD

If you have a friend who you think would benefit from this book, please loan them your copy – or better yet, send them a copy as a gift. I believe (and I hope you do, too) that Millennials desperately need the personal finance skills and knowledge found in this book, so I want to give away as many copies for free as I can – I'm not worried about making money on this book.

So here's the deal: if you gift a copy to a friend who you feel would benefit from this material, send a copy of your Amazon gift receipt and your Venmo handle to *payitforward@money-formillennialsbook.com* and I'll personally reimburse you for your thoughtfulness.

ABOUT THE AUTHOR

Crawford Ifland is the author of *Money for Millennials*, a guide to help Millennials and young twenty-somethings manage their finances wisely and build wealth for the long run. He is passionate about helping others learn more about personal finance, investments, and how to use money wisely.

While in college, Crawford started his first business designing websites for small businesses and non-profits. That part-time stint in college eventually turned into a full-time job. Today, Crawford runs two small creative agencies that specialize in web design and online marketing. His clients include small businesses, award-winning creative artists, venture-backed startups, public and private universities, medical device and biotech companies, private equity firms, and more.

When he is not reading or writing, Crawford enjoys spending time with his wife, drinking coffee, and going to the beach. Crawford is 26 and lives with his wife in sunny Santa Barbara, California.

ACKNOWLEDGMENTS

Thank you to my parents, Rick and Neile Ifland, who instilled in me a healthy view of money as a tool, not the end goal. The wisdom they have passed on through the years has been invaluable to me, and I continue to learn from them every day.

Mom, your advocacy and care for the marginalized and underprivileged is an inspiration and reminds me of what is really important in life. Dad, thank you for encouraging me to see the big picture in every situation, and thank you for offering your discerning eye to help inject life into this manuscript.

Thank you to the many friends and peers who helped me proofread this manuscript and offered their thoughts and reflections. Filipp, Alexandra, Davis, Brooke, Spencer, Jake, Emily, Jim, Dusty, and Trae – I treasure not only your comments and thoughts on this book, but your friendship and mentorship to me over the years. You have helped to shape me into who I am today and have made me a better person – and for that I am deeply grateful.

And of course, thank you to my wonderful wife and best friend, Madeline. You support and encourage me in everything I put my hand to, and I value the insights you have offered as I wrote this book. You are my constant cheerleader, advocate, and daily source of inspiration.

Made in the USA
San Bernardino, CA
05 May 2019